W9-AHO-820

979.4985
J

c-)

THE WIZARD OF SUN CITY

The Strange True Story of Charles Hatfield,
the Rainmaker Who Drowned a City's Dreams

GARRY JENKINS

THUNDER'S MOUTH PRESS

NEW YORK

STAU DISCARD RY

For Thomas, Gabriella, and Cilene

THE WIZARD OF SUN CITY
*THE STRANGE TRUE STORY OF CHARLES HATFIELD, THE RAINMAKER
WHO DROWNED A CITY'S DREAMS*

Published by
Thunder's Mouth Press
An Imprint of Avalon Publishing Group
245 West 17th Street, 11th Floor
New York, NY 10011

AVALON
publishing group incorporated

Copyright © 2005 by Garry Jenkins

First printing July 2005

All rights reserved. No part of this publication may be reproduced or transmitted in any form or by any means, electronic or mechanical, including photocopy, recording, or any information storage and retrieval system now known or to be invented, without permission in writing from the publisher, except by a reviewer who wishes to quote brief passages in connection with a review written for inclusion in a magazine, newspaper, or broadcast.

Library of Congress Cataloging-in-Publication Data is available.

ISBN: 1-56025-675-3

9 8 7 6 5 4 3 2 1

Book design by Jamie McNeely

Printed in the United States
Distributed by Publishers Group West

A believer, a mind whose faith is consciousness, is never disturbed because other persons do not yet see the fact which he sees.

—Ralph Waldo Emerson, *Journals* (1836)

The atmosphere is never at rest. It is one continuous surging mass of humidity, more heavily charged in some spots than in others, thereby causing fogs and clouds, which in time promote or cause rainfall. These conditions have always existed since the beginning of time, and these same conditions will continue to exist as long as this earth lasts.

—Charles Hatfield, promotional brochure (1905)

"Come in!"—the Mayor cried, looking bigger;
And in did come the strangest figure!

—Robert Browning, *The Pied Piper of Hamelin*

CONTENTS

SIGNS

San Diego [December 1915]

"The Moisture Accelerator." Charles Mallory Hatfield, photographed in 1919.
(San Diego Historical Society)

C harles Mallory Hatfield spent the final days of 1915 growing steadily more restless for the turning of the year.

It was a feeling he had experienced before, a niggling knot of impatience that, when he glanced at his pocketwatch, could make him wonder whether time was deliberately dragging its feet. The familiarity didn't make it any easier to bear. Not with so much at stake. Not with the signs he could see gathering around him.

With his younger brother Paul, he had made the hundred-mile train journey from his home at Eagle Rock, near Pasadena, to San Diego, on the Pacific Coast, fifteen miles from the Mexican border, during Christmas week. At first the familiar fragrance of the city—its breezes soft and spiced with the saline sharpness of the ocean, its bustling streets suffused with the scents of gasoline and horse sweat, citrus and fresh-cut lumber—had helped ease his anxieties.

Back in the 1880s, San Diego had been the Hatfields' home, and the journey downtown from the new Santa Fe Railway station on the waterfront evoked warming memories. At the junction of 5th and F streets, the din of newsboys hollering the day's headlines at Hanley's Newsstand took Charles back to the day, in December 1886, when—at the same spot—he had sold sixty-five copies of a special edition of the *San Diego Union* on the death of the Civil War hero John A. Logan. He had been eleven at the time and had run home beaming, his pockets bulging with the extra pennies.

A few blocks away, he saw his old home still standing on the corner of 16th and Broadway. One of three sturdy clapboard dwellings his father had built during the construction boom of 1886, the white house had once dominated the block. But now, with the city in the grip of a new growth spurt and imposing new brick homes springing up in all directions, it seemed a shrunken remnant of another age.

The rude boomtown of Charles's childhood had grown into a place of substance and ambition.

The lobbies of the city's big hotels, the U.S. Grant and the Lincoln, were crammed with tourists from the East, drawn to San Diego by the most spectacular event in the city's history. The Panama California Exposition was intended to capitalize on the city's geographical good fortune as the American port closest to the newly opened Panama Canal. Everywhere were posters proclaiming it the "most beautiful Exposition in the world" and San Diego a "city of miracles." The sense that the city's time had arrived was so tangible, you could almost taste it.

Both Charles and Paul had married San Diego girls—sisters, in fact: Mable and Edna Rulon. The brothers spent their first night back in the city at the home of their in-laws, Jesse and Jennie Rulon, on Kansas Avenue in the well-to-do district of University Heights, at the northeastern corner of the Exposition site in Balboa Park. At dinner the mood was relaxed, the conversation peppered with talk of old times and acquaintances, who-married-who's and whatever-became-of-so-and-so's. Charles slept easily.

It was a change in the weather that jangled his nerves. Charles had arrived in the sort of crisp, clear, shirtsleeve sunshine that—even during winter—set San Diego's boosters rhapsodizing about their "Riviera of the West." By Monday, December 27, however, the temperature had dropped sufficiently for one of San Diego's fanciest stores, Marston's, to start pushing its winterwear collection. The range advertised in the papers that day included "Warm Night Gowns for Women" from 75 cents and men's fur-lined gloves "lined with gray squirrel, beaver and coney" from $5 a pair.

Charles's aging brass-cased barometer bore out Marston's hunch. At sea level, a reading of around 29.8 inches indicated settled weather. The declines the barometer had registered in the past few days were small: a scintilla of an inch here, a fine fraction there. But there was no doubting the quicksilver's progress from Dry and Fair toward Change.

As a gathering of gunmetal gray cumulus massed over the mountains to the southeast, Charles's mood mapped out a similar path. He found himself reaching for his pocketwatch, placing a hand on his ever-present gray felt fedora, and tilting his head to the heavens. . . .

The odd skyward glance aside, few who encountered him would have detected any outward hint of unease.

Charles Hatfield was about five feet nine inches tall, with a build that was wiry, bordering on downright skinny. Volunteering for the army in the Spanish-American War of 1898, he had been rejected as too slight. Now at the age of forty he seemed an even spindlier specimen. His skin was sun-leathered and heavily wrinkled around his eyes when he smiled, which he did often. On the rare occasion when he ventured out hatless, he had a habit of constantly running his fingers through the lank cowlick of hair that flopped across his forehead. The greyhound narrowness of his face was exaggerated by a long, aquiline nose. He was soft-spoken, to the point of diffidence at times. At other times words would gush out in an excited torrent of technical jargon that left his listeners dizzy.

Yet he was possessed of a quiet charisma, a patina of self-confidence that belied his unimpressive physiognomy. On occasion, when he was in full flow, his piercing blue eyes could take on the glaze of the evangelist. "A man on a mission," one acquaintance called him. "Someone who felt right was always on his side," in the words of another friend. Women, in particular, warmed to him. Beneath the surface he harbored every man's share of self-doubt and suspicion. But to the world at large Charles projected an aura so powerful, so charged with positivity, that people believed even Mother Nature herself bent to his will.

In 1915, Charles Mallory Hatfield's name was familiar on four continents. News of his seemingly incredible exploits had been reported from Melbourne to Cape Town, portraits and profiles of him had been published in magazines from New York to London. In Canada he had been the subject of a parliamentary debate. The subject? The government had to decide if allowing him to ply his trade in the northern territories might damage "the vast and delicate atmosphere of the universe." In the past decade the world's newspapers had bestowed upon him an inventive array of names: the "Cloud Compeller," the "God of Plenty," "First Lieutenant to Jupiter Pluvius," and "Professor" Charles Hatfield. Someone had even dubbed him the "Frankenstein of the Air." Few used his preferred description of himself: the "Moisture Accelerator." Most called him Hatfield, the Rainmaker.

Part snake-oil salesman, part pseudoscientist, the rainmaker had woven himself into the legendary fabric of the American West during the frontier's dog days, the 1880s and 1890s. The "profession's" golden age had coincided with a government-financed program to produce artificial rain after a series of droughts that devastated the region from Kansas to California. As a motley collection of charismatics, con men, Washington-backed scientists, and wealthy amateur meteorologists worked their way across the West, the "cloud milkers" found no shortage of farmers desperate for deliverance from their rainless plight.

A few rainmen had enjoyed a moment of fame or, more often, notoriety. A tiny handful were taken seriously by the scientific establishment. None had acquired a prominence—or controversy—to match Charles's, however. It was perhaps the ultimate measure of his success that a thickening file of correspondence on him sat within the Washington offices of the United States Weather Bureau.

His experiments had begun in 1902, at his father's olive ranch at Bonsall, north of San Diego. Charles climbed a windmill tower and mixed a batch of chemicals in a metal pan. Then he lit a fire underneath it and watched the resultant vapor unfurl itself into the atmosphere. Soon thereafter, he claimed, Bonsall—and much of the rest of the county—was doused by an unusually heavy rainstorm.

In the dozen or so years since that day, he had dispensed his "rain stew" into the skies above Los Angeles and Dawson City in the Klondike, and taken credit for breaking droughts as far afield as Texas and Oregon.

As the older generation of rainmakers was discredited and driven from the trade, Charles—uniquely—had stayed in business, not least because he seemed so sincere and straightforward. Throughout his career, Charles maintained that he worked only in conditions where rain already existed in the air. "I do not claim to produce rain from nothing," he would explain in his measured way. "It takes lumber to build a house and it takes flour to make bread. There must be some moisture in the air for me to work on." Which was why, as the New Year drew closer and the barometer's inch-by-fractional-inch decline continued, his expertly masked anxiety deepened with it.

• • •

Charles's impatience had been building for almost three weeks now. He had made an earlier, shorter visit to San Diego on December 11. At a meeting with a committee of councilmen at City Hall, he had presented his proposals for setting up his "precipitation plant" at the largest of San Diego's dams, the vast Morena reservoir, sixty miles outside the city in the Laguna Mountains. They may not have known it, but in passing a motion to accept Charles's plan, the city's burghers had dealt him a doubly precious opportunity. Financially, Charles would enjoy the richest payday of his career—$10,000—if he conjured up enough rain to fill the reservoir. Just as importantly, success at Morena, and the publicity it would bring, might revive a career in danger of becoming becalmed. The euphoria that had coursed through Charles as he left City Hall was tempered only by the realization that time was already against him. Somewhere inside him, a clock had already started ticking.

If there was a subject Charles understood better than any other, it was the rainfall patterns of Southern California in general and San Diego County in particular. It was here that his rainmaking apprenticeship had been served. His desk at Eagle Rock groaned under the weight of detailed weather reports dating back a dozen years and more. He could recite by heart, if necessary, screeds of statistics to prove that the best months for rain in San Diego fell between November and April. He knew he had already missed a month and a half of prime rainmaking time. "As the season is getting late, operations should begin at the earliest convenience," he told the council. The councilmen agreed that he could set up his plant and start work on New Year's Day, 1916. Charles was in such a rush to get going that he left San Diego without tending to the fine print of the contract implied by the council's decision to hire him.

By Tuesday, December 28, Charles and his brother Paul were sweeping around the city with the force of a stiff Santa Ana wind. The barometer had etched another decline that morning, and until the sun had cleared the mountains to the east, there was an enervating sharpness to the morning chill, which drove them on even more.

Six years his brother's junior, Paul routinely downplayed his role in their success. "A flunky," he called himself, but Charles knew the truth. Paul provided a blend of worldliness and muscle he had always lacked. Early in their career, it was Paul who had caught an intruder inside the camp that was their center of operations. "Get out or I'll shoot!" the younger Hatfield had warned the unwelcome guest, looking every inch as if he meant it.

Paul, in turn, was quietly in awe of his brother. He could still recall the wonder he felt when, thirteen years earlier, Charles had first revealed the inventory of raw materials that allowed him to practice his strange trade: an arsenal of dynamite, caps, and gunpowder; a flotilla of tins, pans, scoops, ladles, and long-handled spoons; supplies of timber, tacks, nails, and carpentry equipment; and a stove. Back then it seemed bewildering, the stuff of black magic. Now, however, Paul could calculate the requirements of each assignment by instinct. He did so again.

Paul's first job was to order the lumber to be collected in San Diego en route to Morena. He also oversaw the renting of tents and metal pans, and the ordering of three months' worth of groceries, mainly bacon, sourdough bread, flour, and coffee. The rainmaking chemicals he left to Charles.

While Paul did the rounds of the suppliers, an even more energized Charles strode into City Hall and the Public Works Department with the air of a laird entering his own private fiefdom. "I've got a deal with the city council," he announced. "You've got to get me out to Morena right away."

Personally, the city official he met, John L. Bacon, regarded the so-called rainmaker as nothing more than "a darned good weather prophet." But he had read the reports on the council meeting like everyone else in City Hall. Bacon told Charles that building surveyor H. F. Kirkwood and a works department truck would set them off on their journey up to the Laguna hills the following day, Wednesday.

At around 8:00 A.M. on the morning of Thursday, December 30, Captain Albert Sansom was steering the auxiliary schooner *Allenaire* into the open waters off San Diego when a delegation of nine passengers suddenly appeared on the bridge. From the upper deck they had seen huge green breakers running off the Point Loma headland and panicked. They pleaded with him to turn the vessel around. By 9:00 A.M., only two hours after it had slipped anchor, the *Allenaire* returned to the safety of San Diego Bay and the municipal pier.

The sense that unusually bad weather was around the corner was confirmed that afternoon when the U.S. Weather Bureau issued its forecast for New Year's Eve. "Friday continued cold. Hoist northeastern warning, depression over Southern California, moving southwest."

As was the norm, the forecast drew on information collated at the bureau's Washington headquarters and taken from its thirty weather stations around the United States. Washington believed the front was being caused by unusual conditions in northern Arizona, where a heavy storm had created an area of low pressure. The low had attracted the cold air from a high pressure system formed in the North Pacific and Rocky Mountain states that was now on its way to Southern California, driven by a northeasterly wind. The San Francisco bureau reported heavy frosts in the northernmost parts of the state. Los Angeles and San Diego were expected to suffer the same in the coming days.

Charles did not need a government meteorologist to tell him the band of low pressure was at hand. The long climb up to Morena had taken him southeast of the city along the main state highway to Arizona, through the small hamlets of Jamul, Dulzura, Barrett, and Potrero, across two rivers, Dulzura Creek and the Cottonwood, and on to the border town of Campo, before the final stretch up the corkscrew passes of the Laguna

Range. The journey had done little to quell his impatience. The cloud cover had grown denser and darker all the way. When Charles and Paul emerged from the shelter of the canyons to the exposed higher ground of Morena they found themselves buffeted by high winds.

When Kirkwood and the council workers had unloaded the brothers, they immediately prepared to head back down to San Diego in time for New Year's Eve. Charles hurriedly scratched out a note and sent it back to Kansas Avenue with them. He wrote that, although he was pleased with the spot he'd found, the winds were so disruptive he was having trouble raising his tower. The loss of even more time was annoying, especially given the scale of the job he was undertaking. "However, I will do the best I can."

Amid the revelry of New Year's Eve, the rainmaker's contract barely merited a mention back in San Diego. What serious conversation there was dwelt on the worsening situation in Europe, fresh reports of a British debacle at Gallipoli in Turkey, and, closer to home, the activities of the charismatic bandit Pancho Villa across the border in Mexico. In truth, most San Diegans were too busy congratulating themselves and their city on the year now drawing to a close.

Inaugurating the city's great Exposition a year earlier, on New Year's Day 1915, the event's president and chief cheerleader, G. Aubrey Davidson, had loftily predicted the event would "call the attention of the world to the possibility of millions of acres of land that have been peculiarly blessed by nature and that have awaited through the centuries the touch that will transform them into the paradises of the Western hemisphere." A year later, he had every reason to claim his goal fulfilled.

The throng of parasoled, straw-hatted tourists drawn west during the fair's first months had included Thomas Edison, Henry Ford, William Randolph Hearst, and former president Theodore Roosevelt. Each had agreed it was a show unlike anything else on

"The Most Beautiful in the World." The official seal of the
Panama California Exposition. (San Diego Historical Society)

earth. Inside the fabulous Spanish-flavored Exposition village, the
pastel-colored palacios and prados looked like gaudy wedding
cakes. The fair's attendants were dressed like chocolate soldiers.
Elsewhere people delighted in attractions like the steamship-sized
pipe organ donated by John Spreckels, the city's dominant businessman, electrically operated passenger carts called Electriquettes,
and a scale-model armada of every American warship from John
Paul Jones's *Bonhomme Richard* onward.

The fact that San Diego had been the first city with a population of less than 40,000 people to attempt what was effectively
a world's fair had raised eyebrows across America. Before 1915,

the few Americans who had heard of San Diego thought of it as a trigger-happy frontier town, the last vestige of the old West. By the end of the year thousands had been so taken by the city's climate and bountiful opportunities that they had remained to establish businesses and farms in the surrounding countryside. As 1915 drew to a close, the city's population had climbed to more than 109,000—a "200 per cent increase in four years," according to one booster. New Year's Eve was a time to celebrate the city's success—and toast twelve more months of it.

While the wealthy gathered beneath the bunting and the "Welcome 1916" pennants for a $5-a-plate champagne dinner in the Exposition's ritzy Café Cristobal, the masses converged for a free night of festivities in Balboa Park. The entertainment began with the blowing of the "world's biggest siren whistle." Aubrey Davidson rose to make a speech in which he claimed the final admissions figure for the year had surpassed two million. He also announced that the Exposition would be extended for a second year, this time with a new list of attractions donated by governments around the world. To reflect this, the fair would be renamed the Panama-California *International* Exposition.

Davidson's optimism for the year ahead was boundless. "The eyes of the world are focused on the Sun City and the honor, not only of the great state of California, but of the great West is placed in our keeping," he boomed. "It has long been the most beautiful, it is now the most complete Exposition in the world." To cheers, he predicted that next year's takings would exceed the last and announced his ambition to make San Diego's fair the first in the world to run continuously for two years. "The miracle has been achieved and a greater one is now under way," he promised before signaling to a team of pyrotechnicians.

As the chimes of the park's Spanish clock tower rang out the old year, salvos of silver fireworks illuminated the night. Since before sundown there had been a distinct chill in the air. Ominous clouds had loomed overhead. No sooner had 1916 begun than a light rain started to fall. Few allowed it to dampen the excitement of the moment.

It would be the last time they paid so little heed to the heavens.

For the next thirty days, talk of Pancho Villa and the war—even the great Exposition itself—would be overshadowed. In the space of that month, the city would experience the most extreme weather in its history, a series of storms so strange and intense they seemed to belong in the realm of the supernatural. Lives would be lost; livelihoods would be destroyed; communities would be wiped out. Before it was over, even the city's dreams of greatness would seem to have been washed into the Pacific. If there was talk of miracles, it was conducted in more sinister tones—and attached to the name of the one man whose name was on everyone's lips.

This is the story of Charles Mallory Hatfield, the month that defined his life, and the aberration of nature with which he would forever become associated.

PART I

Rain Wizard [1875–1915]

WHOEVER IT WAS WE'RE GRATEFUL.

"Say Fellers. Who Made the Rain Come?" Cartoon from *Los Angeles Evening Herald,* February 7, 1904.

STORM CHILD

[Fort Scott, Kansas, 1875]

According to the strange and unreliable legend that attached itself to Charles Hatfield's life, even his birth broke a drought. The sole account of his emergence into the world, in Fort Scott, Kansas, on July 15, 1875, claimed it coincided with a monumental cloudburst. The storm announced itself with a lightning bolt that slew four cattle, then sent down rains so tumultuous they transformed the dusty streets into a mud bath, halting the railroad service and stranding a long wagon train heading west from Missouri. It was against this cacophonous backdrop, in her bedroom at 502 Crawford Street, that Marie Mallory Hatfield endured the throes of labor for the third time. It is not hard to imagine that her belief in her second son's divine powers may have been born there, too.

In the absence of any firsthand evidence, only a local news-paper report on the unexpected deluge supports the rickety tale. In that week's edition, the *Fort Scott Weekly Monitor* reported that "the man who predicted a drought this year has been drowned—or ought to be. . . . We will have to have boats to gather the immense corn crop this fall."

It was somehow fitting that what the yarn lacked in details such as facts and provable cause and effect, it more than made up for in mystery, supernaturalism, and pure serendipitous drama. By January 1916 these elements had already woven themselves inextricably into the thread of Charles Hatfield's enigmatic life.

The most celebrated of all rainmakers discovered his calling in California, rather than Kansas. "If I had been a resident of a wet country the thought would never have occurred to me," he often said of the events that changed his life in his midtwenties.

Until then the climate that had shaped him had been an eco-nomic one, an atmosphere measured in real-estate values rather than isobars. His father Stephen Hatfield's passion lay in what his sons called "pioneering" but would be more accurately called property speculation. His endless search for the next boomtown in which to buy, build, and swiftly move on took the young Charles on a restless journey through the emerging mid and far West.

The son of a Quaker blacksmith and farmer from Macedon Center, New York, Stephen Hatfield retained the eighteenth-century traditions of his father's faith. On Sundays he wore the Quaker's buckled, wide-brimmed hat to church meetings where he addressed his brethren in the old-fashioned thees and thous. Then, from Monday to Saturday, he embodied the movement's belief in individualism and self-determination, ideals that inevitably drew him westward.

He had begun his working life as a sewing-machine salesman for the Singer Company, plying his trade in Michigan before heading to the edge of the Great Plains and Davenport, Iowa. It was there in 1869 that he married Marie Mallory, another New

Yorker. Two children, Stephen Girard Hatfield, born in 1870, and Phoebe, born in 1872, soon followed.

By the time he moved to Fort Scott, Kansas, the demands of his expanding family had broadened his horizons. He sold his sewing-machine agency to raise the funds to build a substantial, balconied frame house. By Charles's fifth birthday in 1880, it had been sold at a profit and the family had reestablished itself in Minneapolis.

Stephen's rootlessness created tensions with Marie. "She didn't like it, I guess, at the start," Paul said. But it was hard to argue with the money Stephen was making from his building projects. "He'd buy lots and hire a carpenter to build [on] them." Each sale would generate a few hundred dollars of profit. "It was a pretty good business," said Paul. "She got kind of used to it."

In the end, Marie would be glad to see the back of Minneapolis. Stephen bought land on Nicollet Avenue and erected a house across the road from the Pillsbury flour family. But their six years there were marred by loss. Marie became pregnant three times, but lost two of the children; Frank, aged just two weeks in 1880, and Robert, nine months, in 1884. Only her sixth child, Paul Alden Hatfield, born in June 1886, survived. Within weeks of his birth, the family uprooted itself once more, this time across the Rockies to California and the newest pioneer town: San Diego, the state's original birthplace.

In the 150 years since Spanish priest Father Junipero Serra had placed a cross on what had become known as Presidio Hill, a thriving city had coiled itself around the peardrop contours of the vast, clear-watered inlet he had called the Harbor of the Sun. With San Diego Bay and its port now linked to the rest of the Southwest by the California Southern line to Santa Fe, the greatest growth spurt in the city's short history was under way. In the previous twelve months, property prices had doubled, sometimes tripled. The sight of A-frames being hoisted into place and the noise of ripsaws and hammers filled the alphabetically organized grid of streets that was to become the city's new center. Stephen bought three lots and built three houses at 16th and Broadway. He also bought a forty-acre ranch with an olive grove in Gopher Canyon, near Bonsall, forty or so miles north of the city.

For once his timing was poor. In the spring of 1888, a credit squeeze sparked a stampede out of San Diego. As property prices plummeted, ten thousand people—one-quarter of the city's population—moved on as quickly as they moved in. Most of them went a hundred miles back up the coast to the region's other boomtown, Los Angeles, where the arrival of the Santa Fe Railway had opened up what seemed like a surer opportunity. Stephen joined the exodus that summer, moving Marie and the family once more, this time to a ten-acre ranch with an apricot grove on the corner of Melrose and Vermont avenues in the embryonic community of Hollywood. Of his links to San Diego, only the Bonsall olive ranch remained.

At their new home the Hatfield children were raised to the rhythms of the farming cycle. Paul Hatfield's first memories were of boys baling hay on the farm across the road.

With Stephen, Jr., Charles earned pocket money helping out during the haymaking and crop-harvesting seasons. But his father was adamant that his sons shouldn't waste themselves on farming. While the olives at Bonsall were "big whoppers and beauties" and sold for a good price to an Italian olive oil and pickle manufacturer, the Hollywood apricot crop "didn't amount to much," Paul recalled in later years. Instead, his father steered his sons toward his own first trade.

As boys, both Charles and Paul were experts at dismantling then reassembling the head of a Singer sewing machine. As Charles reached school-leaving age, it became clear he had inherited his father's knack for selling, too.

He had always possessed a quiet charm. It worked wonders on the front porch, particularly with women. "He wasn't a high-pressure salesman. He was very genteel. He had a nice way," his brother Paul remembered. "Everybody liked Charles."

He had another important asset. If he saw doorstep notices that read "No Peddlers," he ignored them and told his customers "I don't believe in signs." By his midtwenties, his quiet persistence had turned him into a star sewing-machine salesman with the Robert Moorehead Agency on South Spring Street in Los Angeles. An average sale was worth $10 to $15. Charles was soon raking in $125 a month, four times the average wage of a manufacturing worker. He spent the money on three-piece pinstripes, silk ties, and fedoras. "He was a dandy," his brother Paul remarked once.

It was his one indulgence. Away from work Charles was reserved and bookish—almost an introvert. "He was a deep thinker, always studying," said Paul. "Especially encyclopedias and books like that." At home his siblings learned to leave him alone when he was submerged in a book. "He didn't want to be bothered."

To his family, Charles's studious nature was the first signal of the ambition within him. The hours he soon began spending in the Los Angeles Public Library at the end of the workday hinted at the dogged determination that he would ally to it. As a member of a farming community in Southern California in the 1890s, it was no surprise that he began to direct those twin forces toward the subject that obsessed his corner of America above all others: the quest for water.

One of the region's founding Franciscan fathers, Juan Crespi, had grasped the harsh geographical reality of the Southern California climate within three weeks of his walking ashore in June 1769. Crespi marched to the heights above San Diego's Mission Bay and saw a land of Edenic qualities, a landscape of willows, poplars, and alders, "Castilian rose bushes with very fragrant roses," wild grapevines, and best of all the San Diego River, "an abundant stream" of "very good, clear water." However, within a month, a relentless sun had transformed a raging river into a shrunken stretch of mud that Father Crespi's men could cross "dry shod." "If this continues it will be necessary to look for another place to establish the mission and establish irrigation," he wrote.

The Spanish settlers soon learned that the indigenous natives, the Duiegans, had their own explanation for the region's rainless nature. The Duiegans worshiped Chinigchinix, a vengeful deity who had created man out of mud then retired to heaven from where he doled out cruel punishments to those who sinned. Deep in history, a riled Chinigchinix had unleashed a great tide of water that consumed everything before it. Their land would never be drowned again, they told one of the Spanish settlers, "because Chinigchinix does not wish there will be another flood."

No one who settled in the arid landscape found cause to question the legend.

The Spanish quickly grasped that surviving the dry years depended on saving the excess rainfall—or "runoff"—from the wet ones and used their corps of native Indians to construct an ingenious system of cisterns, wells, and miniature reservoirs capable of storing up to 70,000 gallons. In 1814 they had surpassed themselves by spanning a stretch of the San Diego River with a 250-foot-wide dam connected (via a six-mile aqueduct made of tiles, stones, and cement) to the Spanish mission.

By 1890, the region boasted mountain dams and epic flumes. San Diego's first dam, the Cuyamaca, was connected to the city by a conduit that stretched sixty miles into the mountains. Yet as Charles could see all too clearly, the region's chronic lack of reliable water continued to hobble its progress.

Both at Bonsall and Los Angeles, dry spells were, as Charles put it, "a terrible menace to the agricultural and stock-raising interests." Dams and wells ran dry regularly. The little water that did remain in the ground could be too alkaline to drink. The Hatfields' apricot and olive crops suffered often, and so did the region at large. As a teenager, Charles heard talk of defaulted loans, repossessed land, and suicides among farmers. The sadness of these stories made a deep impression. Even more powerful, however, was the talk he began to hear of men with the power to break open the unyielding heavens.

WAR AND THE WEATHER

[Southern California, 1886–1900]

The first of the artificial rain schemes to circulate the farming communities of Southern California was generally discussed in a whisper and with a faintly pitying smile.

By the 1880s the state had already become a magnet for cultists and bohemians. One of its new arrivals, an artist named Michael Cahill, believed that rain clouds were formed by high-flying birds such as eagles and condors, which "open vents for the vapor to ascend and form clouds, like escape valves from steam engines." To harness their energy, he proposed the federal government breed, tame, and train four to six pairs of birds for every 100 square miles of the country. These could then be released during dry spells "so as to give timely rain." Amazingly, the California legislature allowed him "informal hearings" in

1886. A few hours in his company and the lawmakers were siding with the newspaper editorial that had dismissed Cahill as "a crazy loon."

The episode spoke volumes about the seriousness of the region's ongoing irrigation problems. The decade and a half that followed offered up a plentiful supply of alternative rainmaking schemes for it to consider—almost all of them saner than Cahill's birdbrained plan.

Theirs was not the first generation to believe they could milk the skies. The Hopi danced and the Iroquois burned tobacco. In Africa, Asia, and Australia, tribesmen spat water into the air, covered themselves in bird down and fresh blood, and performed a ritual involving the circumcised foreskins of young boys to deliver downpours. In eighteenth-century Europe, the sight of swollen clouds overhead sent bell ringers running to the nearest church tower. The theory was that the clamorous noise could shake the moisture loose. In England so many bell ringers were killed by lightning that the practice was officially banned.

Yet never had the notion of artificial rain been regarded with the scientific earnestness that it was in the America of the late-nineteenth century.

It was a period of supreme confidence. Back East, Thomas Edison and Henry Ford were transforming improbable technology into the stuff of everyday living. In their bicycle repair shop in Dayton, Ohio, Orville and Wilbur Wright were preparing to make the most miraculous step of all. It was the era of technology, of practical miracles, of Progress. Necessity had always been the mother of American invention. With the mid and far West blighted by droughts, serious-minded men were convinced artificial rain would be science's next great breakthrough.

The most promising work was being conducted away from the public gaze. In Chicago, an inventor named Louis Gathmann had noticed that when artillery shells exploded at high altitudes, they formed clouds in their wake. He was sure that rain and snow were formed by the cooling of moist air to its dewpoint, and in 1891 he patented a shell containing liquid carbonic-acid gas that could supercool the atmosphere. Elsewhere a University of Texas physicist, Lucien Blake, was dusting the skies with "smoke balls" made of turpentine mixed with sawdust, released via high-altitude balloons. His idea was based on the widely accepted theory that saturated water vapor particles needed something solid to attach themselves to in order to condense into droplets of rain. His "smoke balls" would act as a stimulus.

In both cases, the science was solid. In both cases, however, it was far ahead of its time. In the early part of the 1890s, it was another, more straightforward idea that took hold of the public's imagination—and its purse strings. For some time, America placed its faith in Robert St. George Dyrenforth's ability to literally blow the moisture out of the skies.

Plutarch was the first to link war and the weather. In his history of the war between the Roman general Marius and the Teutons in 104–101 B.C., the historian wrote that "extraordinary rain pretty generally falls after great battles: whether it be that some divine power thus washes and cleanses the polluted earth with showers from above, or that moist and heavy evaporation streaming forth from blood and corruption thicken the air."

The idea had lingered in the minds of military men ever since. To some it explained the storms that handicapped the Spanish armada at Trafalgar and caused the mud that undid Napoleon at Waterloo. Napoleon himself gave the idea credence in France. In 1831, massed ranks of French artillery men fired thousands of rounds in an attempt to stimulate approaching thunderclouds. But it was in drought-afflicted America that the percussion theory found its moment at last.

Its revival was launched by a book, *War and the Weather: The Artificial Production of Rain*, in which Chicago civil engineer Edward Powers, chronicled some two hundred Civil War battles that, he claimed, had been fought in the face of falling rain. Powers found thousands of both Union and Confederate supporters.

By 1890 farmers were seizing on rumors of successful experiments in Europe, where French vintners had taken to firing at clouds to produce rain for their grape crops. In Montana, a Reverend L. B. Woolfolk used his pulpit to ask Washington why this technology wasn't being employed to save his drought-hit flock. "By the firing of cannon balls" the prairies could enjoy "one perpetual summer."

Washington's professional weathermen pooh-poohed the idea. "About as effective as booing a blizzard," a U.S. Weather Bureau official, William Humphrys, called it. Yet by 1891 Congress was approving an initial $7,000 "for experiments in the production of rainfall" and appointing Dyrenforth to run them.

A decorated Union soldier with a Ph.D. from the University of Heidelberg, Dyrenforth proposed exploding balloons filled with a high-combustion mix of oxygen and hydrogen and "rackarock," an innovative new explosive made of potassium chlorate and petroleum, at high altitudes. His thinking was that the detonating bombs would produce "something in the nature of a vortex or of a momentary cavern, into which the condensed moisture is drawn from afar or falls." The effect of this, he thought, "may squeeze the water out of the air like a sponge."

Dyrenforth's tests were taken so seriously that detailed reports of his experiments ran in newspapers across the nation. In his rain-starved corner of the country, Charles Hatfield devoured every scrap.

Dyrenforth did not get off to the most auspicious start. His first test, at Piney Branch outside Washington, D.C., merely proved that the "rackarock" made a hellish noise and that loud explosions played havoc with the nerves of livestock. The chief clerk of the Smithsonian Institution phoned Dyrenforth to harangue him about the effect it had on his thoroughbred Jersey cattle.

He fared a little better in August when he attacked the skies above Midland, Texas. Twelve hours later, rain fell.

When news of the first rain reached Washington, newspapers declared "They Made Rain" and "Made the Heavens Leak." His supporters in Congress were soon talking about turning $1 million over to his rainmaking brigade. It didn't last long.

Dyrenforth's next two tests—in Santa Fe and then in Corpus Christi—again achieved poor results. At his next experiment in San Antonio, Texas, Dyrenforth used a new, even more powerful explosive, "rosellite," to blow up his balloons and kites. But this time there was next to no rain recorded. There was also a platoon of professional meteorologists and physicists on hand to vouch for the fact.

Slowly, doubting articles appeared in farming newspapers in Chicago and Dallas. By the time Dyrenforth's westward progress brought him to San Diego, Texas, the press back East had turned on him. The *Washington Post* reported that on one night Dyrenforth exploded a dozen balloons, 175 shells, and 1,200 charges of rosellite. "And yet the whole hullabaloo did not lead to any more water than would furnish a canary bird with its morning bath." The *Chicago Times* thought the money would have been better spent on "the attempted manufacture of whistles out of pig's tails." A wag in one newsroom came up with a new epithet: "Dryhenceforth."

His experiments continued for a few more months, but the writing was on the wall. Soon Washington was breaking the news that funding for his experiments had been stopped. Privately, concussionist experiments would continue for another decade and more. But the government would not risk the opprobrium again.

The skies may have resisted, but the teenage Charles Hatfield did not. Dyrenforth's exploits made an indelible impression, so much so that Hatfield referred to the cloud bomber in reverential tones throughout his career. Hatfield also remained reluctant to accept that Dyrenforth's experiments were as misguided as history claimed: "I may say that this disturbance of the atmosphere by explosions, at the higher height the better, is an old but in many cases successful method," he would say, while at the same time denying any suggestion he adhered to the "rackarock school" of rainmaking. It would not be a distance he could so easily maintain from America's next great cloud milker, Clarence B. Jewell, especially as Jewell was operating on Charles's doorstep.

To the hundreds of curious Los Angelenos who crowded along a length of railway siding at the edge of the city in July 1899, the sight before them must have seemed like something straight out of the fervid imagination of Jules Verne.

Dominating the railyard was a giant transcontinental locomotive, just in from the East and marked out in the livery of the Chicago, Rock Island, and Pacific Railway (CRIPR). What really caught the eye, however, was the boxcar coupled to the engine. While the front end of the car had been converted into an ornately decorated accommodation cabin and dining carriage, the rear section had been mysteriously blacked out and had a tall stovepipe funnel protruding from its roof. Barking orders to his team of eccentric-looking assistants from the deck at the rear of the boxcar was an earnest figure in a suit and hat. Few of those gathered around the track got close enough to see the face of Clarence B. Jewell, the famed "wizard of the Rock Island Railroad." The stench emanating from the stovepipe was too great.

Even by Southern California's arid standards the drought that had begun in 1897 was severe. Wells all over the region had run dry. Water companies were forced to drill into the rock-hard riverbeds to open new wells. Even the dams emptied out. By the summer of 1898 the Cuyamaca had been reduced to a cracked and barren bowl. So perhaps it was inevitable that the region would turn to the man who had replaced Dyrenforth as America's best-known rainmaker.

Jewell was working as a dispatcher for the CRIPR when he joined the rainmaking ranks in 1892. Fate sent him to the railroad depot in Goodland, Kansas, the town that had—almost accidentally—become the nexus of the Midwest's burgeoning rainmaking industry the previous year. By 1891, Goodland had no less than three full-time rainmaking companies operating within its city limits, each of them practicing the so-called "smell-making method" of inducing rain, each of them guarding their secret as if it were the most valuable on earth.

It was hardly a secret at all.

Again, the notion stretched back to the ancients. The Greek historian Thucydides was the first to link large fires with rain. So had eighteenth-century Jesuits, who, while traveling in Paraguay, watched native Indians successfully torch their prairies to stimulate rain. The German scientist and traveler Alexander von Humboldt had connected erupting volcanoes with the subsequent formation of clouds, thunderstorms, and "violent rain." Yet the practical inspiration behind Jewell's method had come from one of America's most revered scientific minds.

The rainmaking industry virtually owed its existence to James Pollard Espy. Espy had been at the heart of the celebrated quest for the Law of Storms half a century earlier. The public debates on the causes of the American continent's unique range of storms pitted Espy against two other meteorological eminences, William C. Redfield and Robert Hare. Their exchanges were dominated by five questions. The four more esoteric ones related to electricity in the air, tornadoes, the gyratory power of spouts and whirlwinds, and the trade winds. But the fundamental question concerned rain: What caused it?

Almost everyone agreed it began with the evaporation of the earth's oceans, lakes, and rivers into the atmosphere. The question was how this water vapor was transformed into rain droplets that were sent back to earth. Hare sided with the eighteenth-century theory of James Hutton, which stated that rain was caused by the overrunning and mixing of currents of vapor-saturated air of different temperatures. Redfield didn't think it that simple and put it down to "numerous causes" from an absence of the sun's rays to "vortical gyrations." Espy's argument cited upward-moving columns of moist air that released what he called "the steam power of the atmosphere."

After a decade of argument, the trio emerged agreeing on a few accepted principles, such as the differences between hurricanes, tornadoes, and thunderstorms. Yet the answer to the greatest question eluded them. Not for the last time, the scientific establishment reluctantly agreed that the atmosphere was simply too vast and unpredictable to explain. It was a truth that had served the scientific rainmaking movement for fifty years.

Espy was also rainmaking's most respected advocate. Like Humboldt, he had noted how rainfall seemed higher over volcanoes, fuel-burning cities, and accidental fires. Encouraged by experiments using a pioneering instrument, the "nephelscope," a forerunner of the modern cloud chamber, he wondered whether it might be possible to create clouds—and rainfall—by artificially raising a large, well-directed column of warm air.

Espy called on the government to build a network of vast, forty-acre bonfires, stretching six or seven hundred miles north to south. The pyre complex should be built somewhere in the Midwest, where it could be burned every week throughout the summer. The result, he predicted, would be a "rain of great length, north and south" that would travel eastward to the Atlantic, eliminating all droughts, increasing "the proceeds of agriculture," and enhancing "the health and happiness of the citizens." Espy argued that the scheme would cost U.S. citizens no more than half a cent per year. Its rejection by Washington had spurred a generation of dreamers and amateur rainmakers.

In Texas an inventor came up with a novel machine—the "Rainolette"—designed to blow a column of warm air thousands of feet into the atmosphere. In New York, inventor G. H. Bell proposed a stone tower 1,000 feet tall with a wooden or iron tower extending a further 500 feet on top. The tower would be hollow and would allow a reversible blower to pump hot air into the upper reaches so as to summon an Espy Shower. A similar idea was proposed by John Jacob Astor IV. Although each of these ideas foundered, a more pragmatic breed of rainmaker soon emerged to put Espy's methods to work.

The father of the so-called "fume men" was "the Australian wizard" Frank Melbourne.

Melbourne was, in fact, an Irishman who had arrived in America via sojourns in New Zealand and Australia, where he claimed to have developed a rainmaking formula so powerful it had caused a major flood that forced him to flee the country and its irate farmers. Tall, mustached, and handsome, with a taste for wine, women, and monogrammed shirts, Melbourne's flair for mingling salesmanship with burlesque led one observer to call him a "kind of cornfield Barnum."

To preserve the mystery of his process, Melbourne kept his rainmaking machine in a black gripsack he called "the baby" and guarded it day and night with a large revolver. At work he would disappear into a cubicle, shed, or loft, from where "a rumbling, fluttering sound" would emerge before black smoke seeped out from the cracks. His method, it later transpired, was based on a blend of Espy's idea and elementary chemistry. He created a simple column of hydrogen by adding zinc to muriatic acid.

In June 1891, in Cheyenne, the governor of Wyoming offered Melbourne $150 to produce 1.5 inches of rain within three days. On the second day, there were violent thunderstorms. Lightning killed four cattle belonging to one of the committeemen who had hired him, but he was paid nevertheless. Melbourne and his bookmaker brother, Will, made ten times their fee in bets. He was soon winning contracts all over the Midwest.

To his doubters, Melbourne was simply a clever player of the law of averages. A professor of physics at Texas University was appalled at how by releasing "some colored gas through a small pipe in the roof" Melbourne could persuade even supposedly intelligent people that he was manipulating the heavens. His suspicions were confirmed when someone noticed that the days Melbourne picked for producing rain coincided exactly with the predictions in the popular farmer's almanac published by Irl R. Hicks of St. Louis.

The end was tawdry. Melbourne was found dead in a scruffy Denver hotel room in 1894. The body was identified only through an F.M. monogram on some of his belongings. The official verdict was suicide, although rumors of skulduggery, rival rainmakers, and a stolen formula soon swirled.

Many were convinced that Clarence Jewell had acquired his secret.

In the spring of 1892, Jewell had asked his bosses at the railway for $250 to buy rainmaking chemicals. His success in breaking a drought nearby persuaded them that giving Jewell a full-time job as a rainmaker might be "in the interest of science." The fact that good crops meant good freight business was hardly incidental, of course. Soon his specially converted boxcar was touring Kansas, Nebraska, and Oklahoma, drawing crowds to compete with the great traveling circuses of Barnum and Adam Forepaugh back East. He enjoyed a longevity none of his rivals could match and was even invited to Chicago's World's Fair in 1893.

Jewell guarded his secret formula just as closely as Melbourne had. Charles M. Sheldon, a Topeka minister who was one of the few to get inside Jewell's boxcar, described a complex mechanical and electrical apparatus so baffling it was "as if they had been the stock in trade of a necromancer." What was clear was that the equipment generated gas that was pumped out into the stovepipe via a huge overhead tank containing some 800 gallons of water. Jewell told Sheldon he pumped 1,500 feet of gas every hour and that the plumes reached as high as 8,000 feet.

Jewell, although a "quiet, urbane gentleman," understood the power of showmanship. At times he indulged in Dyrenforth-style rocketry. One contemporary described how he fired a "monster mortar . . . a sort of cross between a cannon of exceptionally large caliber and a giant slingshot." The weapon hurled chemical bombs that would explode a confetti of yellow smoke 1,000 feet in the air.

Mostly, however, he stuck to the less spectacular, though no less peculiar, art of fume raising. It was this that he concentrated on during his visit to Los Angeles in July 1899.

The ritual that the city witnessed that month had been best described a few years earlier by a correspondent of *Harper's Magazine*.

One of Jewell's assistants was a small hunchback. "The little stooped man climbed the iron ladder to the roof of the car where he studied the sky—we held our breath. Then he sent out word that 'the sky was right.'

"Next, a great stirring inside the mysterious car, and, in a few minutes, a grayish gas began coming out of the stovepipe hole in the roof. In no time the gas hit our noses—the most evil smelling stuff we had ever encountered."

The *Harper's* man went on to describe the central dilemma that faced anyone hoping to prove or disprove the effectiveness of men like Jewell. Forty-eight hours after he witnessed Jewell's vaudevillian act, he felt a light rain. But who was to say what caused it? God, Mother Nature, or the Wizard of the Rock Island Railway?

As it turned out, in Los Angeles it was an academic question.

Jewell set to work toward the end of the month. His assistant climbed to the roof, announced that the "skies were right," and the vast water tank began bubbling away. A light breeze soon bore the "evil smelling stuff" across the Hatfield apricot grove and beyond into the Hollywood hills.

In all, Jewell spent sixty continuous hours pumping slate-colored gas from the stovepipe. Throughout that time the skies remained a resolute milky blue.

Jewell had been hired by the city's chamber of commerce. The businessmen soon lost their patience and demanded the rain-maker return his fee. By August, his leviathan locomotive had trundled back East. His career came off the tracks soon thereafter.

But it was not quite the last the region would hear from him.

Six months after Jewell's departure, in January 1900, dozens of Western newspapers ran reports claiming to have discovered his secret formula. The *San Diego Union* was among them. According to the *Union's* report, all an amateur "cloud milker" had to do was mix "Ten fluid ounces of sulphuric acid, five ounces of zinc and 50 fluid ounces of water" in a metal pan, then "renew every hour and stir every thirty minutes day and night until rain begins to fall." Hardware stores were soon running short of supplies of each ingredient, and within days, two prominent San Diego businessmen—John Mumford and John Capron—announced they were building four rainmaking stations to test the formula. They thought it their civic duty to give the Jewell formula a whirl. Between them they spent a small fortune on 1,600 pounds of acid and 400 pounds of zinc.

The two men erected four wooden towers in early February. They followed the Jewell method to the letter, but by February 12 they were arguing publicly over the lack of results. Capron blamed Mumford for getting the formula wrong. Mumford reckoned it was Capron who had fouled up. By the time the rainmaking stations were dismantled and abandoned a few days later, it emerged that the church had been instrumental in persuading at least one of the pair to quit. "You are tempting God to visit all kinds of evil on San Diego," Capron had been told by one pastor.

People drew the conclusions they wanted from the debacle.

To the doubters, it confirmed that Jewell and company were one step removed from the traveling hucksters who sold cough cures, lightning rods, and miracle seeds. Indeed, they argued, the medicine salesmen were playing precisely the same percentage game. Their medical dictionaries told them that in 80 percent of cases, humans recovered from an illness regardless of whether or not they were treated. They sided with an editorial in the magazine *Irrigation Farmer* in which the rainmaker was dismissed as "a fraud, an ingenious tramp who played upon the cupidity and superstitions of the people and worked them the same as a slight-of-hand performer."

Yet with the Southern California drought showing no sign of abating, there were plenty who retained their faith in American science and believed that the answer remained out there—somewhere. Stubbornly they clung to the hope expressed by a midwestern newspaper editorial at the height of the drought: "Many frauds will bloom out in the rain-making business, but out of the seekers, out of notoriety will eventually come forth one Edison, a wizard."

"THREE HUNDREDTHS OF AN INCH"
[Bonsall, 1902]

Hauling himself out of bed at Bonsall, California, on April I, 1902, Charles felt the unusual chill of the morning and went straight to the window. He saw ribbons of dense gray sea mist draping themselves over the valleys to the west. Within moments he was outside, breathing in the clammy coldness of the new day.

Charles had spent hours waiting for the opportunity he now saw. He hurriedly began hauling equipment up and down the windmill tower. Soon, on a platform thirty-odd feet off the ground, he had arranged a small group of metal pans into which he poured a ready-mixed blend of chemicals and water. Giving the mixture a final stir, he placed an electric heater underneath the pans and sat back as a plume of vapor began rising, wraith-like, into the moist morning air.

To the naked eye the column of heated air was almost imperceptible. To the nose, it was an affront. Charles placed himself upwind so as to avoid being overwhelmed by the stench.

He spent most of the morning regularly stirring and replacing the chemicals. Before long a fog drifted over the ranch, merging into the low-level stratus cloud already hanging overhead. By noon a thin but steady rain was falling. It continued for more than an hour. When the showers abated he checked—and rechecked—his rain gauge, barely able to suppress the smile on his face. "Got three hundredths of an inch of rain," he remembered many times afterward. "I surprised myself."

Hatfield began his "deep and serious study of the science of the atmosphere" a year or so after the great Southern California drought began.

At the library he found two books more illuminating than the rest: John Brocklesby's *Elements of Meteorology, with Questions for Examination, Designed for Schools and Academies* (1848), and, in particular, *Elementary Meteorology* (1894) by William Morris Davis, the standard book on the weather in America at the time. He bought copies of both. His battered and heavily annotated editions would remain part of his library for the next fifty years.

It is easy to see how Davis's grandiose opening statement would have fired Charles's imagination. "We dwell on the surface of the land; we sail across the surface of the sea; but we live at the bottom of the atmosphere. Its changes pass over our heads; its continual fluctuations control our labors," he wrote with mysterious gravity.

Yet as he delved into the science of that atmosphere, Charles discovered a discipline still struggling to agree upon its most fundamental principles. It had been a century of startling theoretical breakthroughs. Gustave Gaspard Coriolis had noticed the effect the earth's rotation has on its wind patterns, causing winds to travel clockwise around high-pressure systems in the Northern Hemisphere and counterclockwise in the Southern. With the century's last gasps, the Frenchmen Teisserenc de Bort had sent barometer-bearing balloons into the upper reaches and deduced that there must be a new layer of atmosphere—the stratosphere —between 29,000 and 45,000 feet up. But the practical mysteries of the weather remained as elusive as ever. Half a century after the Law of Storms debate, universal agreement on the source of rain remained out of reach.

On the subject of rain, Davis's book reflected the confusion that still endured. He offered a medley of causes, leaning toward the Hutton school of currents overlapping and mixing, and Espy's "steam power." He was clearer on the subject of artificial rainmaking: "Observations thus far made do not give encouragement to these projects," he wrote of Dyrenforth and the fume men. After the experience of April 1, Charles begged respectfully to differ. He was sure he had come up with another approach to the problem altogether.

Like James Watt, the father of steam locomotion, Charles found inspiration in a boiling kettle. In his mother's kitchen one day, he noticed the kettle's steam seemed to attract the water vapor rising from a pan on an adjacent stove. It set him thinking about whether it would be possible to release a chemical equivalent of that steam that would somehow draw in rain-laden clouds.

The idea, as Charles saw it, amounted to a form of meteorological magnetism. "It is a mere matter of cohesive attraction and the conditions that produce rain are drawn by my system just as a magnet draws steel," he would come to say of his "beautiful theory." "I merely attract the clouds and they do the rest." Charles had always seen an incongruity in San Diego's weather. Although rain was scarce, the readings he took with his hygrometer indicated an atmosphere thick with moisture. The potential was there—all he needed to do was unlock it.

The fogs that came in off the coast at Bonsall offered an obvious opportunity to test the idea. The way the fog had drifted toward his tower—then dissolved into a fine rain—had validated his thinking. A more skeptical mind would perhaps dismiss it as a happy coincidence, a natural corollary of the conditions. For Charles it could be no such thing. He was onto something "unique, unlike anything seen before."

In practical terms, the similarities between Charles and his fume-raising predecessors were obvious—despite his protestations otherwise. Charles always maintained that his chemical formula was different from anyone else's. He once let slip that it consisted of twenty-seven different chemicals, even though the circumstantial evidence linking his formula to Clarence Jewell's would grow stronger over the course of his career. Yet, in at least two senses, he was unique. What distinguished his method from those of his rivals was not delivery but direction, the weather conditions in which he set up and operated his towers. That and the fact that he was soon producing results beyond anything American rainmaking had yet witnessed.

At the sewing-machine agency, Charles's boss, Robert Moorehead, gave his star salesman plenty of room. Provided he made the sales, Moorehead didn't much mind the hours he kept or what he got up to away from the office. As the summer approached, Charles took full advantage of the situation and headed down to Bonsall at every opportunity.

He'd told no one about the April 1 experiment. He even maintained his vow of silence after a second successful test in May. "Well sir, I got 0.04—an 0.01 more," he recalled years later.

His family's suspicions were aroused by his secretiveness, however. By July he couldn't contain himself any longer. He'd run his third test during what was, in theory at least, the driest month of the year. "On that occasion it rained 0.65 of an inch, a record never before nor since equaled for a July in that county."

Back in Los Angeles, he revealed what he'd been up to. He was being honest with himself by now too. The third test at Bonsall marked the moment he saw a new course opening up for himself. As he put it later: "I knew I had something."

SOME DIVINE POWER

[Los Angeles, 1903–1904]

Although Stephen Hatfield, Sr. did not approve of his son's strange weather-taunting tests—he once called them "a foolish waste of valuable time"—this view was far from universal within the Hatfield home. In England the Quaker movement had been forged in a climate of fevered mysticism and miracle making, much of it stirred up by their charismatic seventeenth-century founder, George Fox. At the dawn of the twentieth century the belief in "inner light," of "God being within," remained strong within the Society of Friends. Marie Hatfield saw it at work within Charles. "My mother thought that it was kind of an act of God. She said it must have been a divine providence. That God was kind of helping him out through some unknown power," his brother Paul said. Her faith was rooted in the strange and unearthly events of January 1904.

In the late summer of 1903, Stephen sold the house on Melrose Avenue to "a couple of rich widows from Pittsburgh." He decided to get rid of the home in Bonsall at the same time. The healthy profit enabled him to buy a whole block of houses in Inglewood, northeast of Los Angeles.

His decision to sever all ties with farming was predictable. The drought was now entering its seventh year. All over Southern California, newspaper talk of parched cropland and cattle dying of starvation had become depressingly familiar. "The air bore clouds of dust," one city newspaper reported that winter. Panic was setting in, even among those with longer memories. "This is the first time since 1872 that we have not had any green grass at this time of the year," mourned Jotham Bixby, one of Long Beach's biggest cattle barons.

By the end of January 1904, there seemed little option but to summon divine intervention. The city's clergymen declared Sunday, January 31, a day of prayer for rain. The churches bulged, the sermons thundered, but the congregations emerged to skies as wan and cloudless as ever.

Two days later, on February 2, a horse-drawn wagon pulled Charles, Paul, and a cargo of lumber up into the brush country at the base of the mountains in La Crescenta. By evening, the first fires were burning beneath the chemical trays.

It was, in fact, their second trip to the mountains.

Charles had got the idea of heading to the hills from his meteorological bible, Davis's *Elementary Meteorology*. Davis had written that "because the dew-point to which the air is cooled by the various processes of cloud-making is most commonly encountered at this altitude . . . the greatest measure of rainfall in a given region is not at sea level or at the level of the earth's surface, but at a certain moderate altitude in the atmosphere." Davis believed the ideal height was around 4,000 feet above sea level.

Charles had ordered enough lumber to construct a tower similar in size to the windmill at Bonsall. His only problem now was practical. He needed an extra pair of hands, and it was only natural that he turned to his younger brother Paul.

For the seventeen-year-old, the experience was "wild," a taste of real pioneering as it had been lived only a decade or two earlier. In keeping with the Western tradition, the brothers helped themselves to an empty cabin, sat out under the stars making popcorn, and burned gallon after gallon of chemicals. After three and a half days, a small amount of rain fell. The normally taciturn Charles headed down the mountain talking ten to the dozen, his brother later remembered. "He was very elated," said Paul.

The second trip was the idea of Charles's boss, Robert Moorehead. Back at the agency, Charles had talked openly about his successes for the first time. Moorehead was a gambler and a racehorse owner and quickly bit. By January he had convinced a group of businessmen—mainly shoe-store owners—to put up a prize of $50.

Their departure for the hills brought Charles his first piece of publicity. "Rainmaker Hatfield is a sewing machine solicitor by day. By night he delves into the mysteries of penumbra and cirrus, air strata and all the queer habits of the realm above," the *Los Angeles Herald* reported on Wednesday, February 3. It quoted Charles as telling the businessmen that he could bring an inch of rain in the next five days for $50. As Paul never tired of recalling afterward, Charles did the job in exactly "two days, two hours and ten minutes."

Just as Charles had hoped, a heavy fog rolled in on Thursday. At the tower, he and Paul went into overdrive, almost knocking themselves out on the fumes from the chemical tank. By 6:00, a hard and insistent rain was falling. By midnight, unthinkable volumes of water were running in the streets.

The rain was not confined to Los Angeles. From San Luis Obispo in the north to Anaheim in the south, around three-quarters of an inch fell. All across Southern California, scenes mirrored those in Los Angeles, where "staid businessmen capered like schoolboys . . . fair women forgot their costly gowns . . . even the blasé cabbies sat up and began to take notice."

A visiting businessman, Fred Rothschilds of the Canadian Klondike Company, was taken aback at the scene. "The rain certainly was unstrained," he recalled. "It brought down fishes and gravel and heavy stones. The gutters choked and sewers were above the plimsoll mark. I had to wade against an uphill stream that struck me above the knees. Talk about rain."

While the churches began thanksgiving services, the newspapers returned to the far more intriguing story of the young "drought destroyer." Reporters were dispatched to find the enigma, and editorials openly wondered whether he was responsible.

HATFIELD MAY CLAIM CREDIT FOR THE PRECIPITATION, ran one headline. "In answer to the prayers of the church, as a result of Rainmaker Hatfield's machinations or from natural causes, rain began falling . . ." began the *Los Angeles Herald*'s open-minded report.

From his sixth-floor office in the Trust Building, the chief of the Los Angeles office of the United States Weather Bureau, George E. Franklin, moved fast to dampen any notions of otherworldly intervention. Franklin himself had been caught napping by the rain. He had noticed a drop in pressure and talked of conditions being right, but predicted the rain would be diverted eastward. The storm was the "tail end of a storm that swept down from the Oregon coast with great rapidity," he told the *Herald*.

Franklin was quick to caution those who believed Charles and his "chemical affinity" was responsible. "I would not say that the preachers or the rainmaker is responsible for the rain. Personally I am inclined to think we should thank that power which for decades past has controlled such things," he said. "It seems queer to me that a man by a chemical assault on the heavens in the foothills in Southern California should be responsible for a storm which began way up on the Oregon coast."

Few paid Franklin much attention.

• • •

Charles came down from La Crescenta to find himself feted as a miracle worker.

He and Paul were picking up supplies from a corner store when they saw the *Los Angeles Times*. Along with a photograph of their tower sat a picture of their mother.

Her words dominated the page: "The people's prayers for rain have been answered through my son. For five years he has studied and struggled against prejudices. His determination is simply marvelous. Some divine power must aid him."

It turned out the reporter had been looking for Charles, but his mother had sent him on a wild-goose chase.

Charles happily entertained the next visitor, a reporter from the *Times*'s rival, the *Herald*. In his first interview, the "cloud compeller" came across as an earnest mixture of scientist and philanthropist. He also adopted a habit he would maintain for life: talking a lot but giving away very little. He explained that his method was "a purely scientific process" in which he produced rain "by means of effect on the atmosphere of the evaporation of certain chemicals." He was adamant that his formula remain a secret. From the outset, however, he made it clear that—unlike some of the charlatans of the past—he did not claim to summon rain from clear blue sky. "All I have to demand for success is that there should be some humidity in the air," he said. "I do not fight nature, I woo her by natural means."

He sympathized with those who had prayed for rain. "I noticed that the ministers of the city prayed for rain on Sunday and all they got were a few clouds on Monday," he said. "Many of my own ancestors were clergymen, and the Rev. George T. Dowling of this city is my cousin: but in this case I think science, as far as producing rain goes, is ahead of praying." Charles claimed his operation at La Crescenta had been a loss maker, costing him $100, even after the $50 reward. But he offered to unleash his chemicals again "any time anyone wishes at any place." His return to selling sewing machines for Robert Moorehead was short-lived.

By the following December, the region's wells were running dry once more. This time, encouraged by the *Los Angeles Examiner*, Charles made a public proposition. In return for $1,000, he would guarantee 18 inches of rain between mid-December and late April. The money would be deposited with the paper. If he failed, it would be returned to the subscribers, and he would bear the losses—of expenses and reputation.

Charles and Paul set up their camp on the grounds of a sanitarium at Esperanza, near Altadena. They began what Charles promised would be "an all winter siege" on December 15. A week later, on Thursday, December 23, a sudden downpour deposited the first 0.39 inches.

The rain's arrival did nothing for the mood of George Franklin at the weather bureau, who had predicted clear conditions. "I am inclined to believe it came from the sea. Storms from there come without a moment's notice," he snapped when asked if he thought Charles was responsible. "Hatfield is working for that $1,000. We at the weather bureau are working for the good of the people at low wages."

Charles put out a statement, too. It simply said: "I did it and the rain will continue until Thursday afternoon."

The rain magnet drew crowds to Esperanza. Those who traveled up from Los Angeles expecting monstrous black clouds of smoke and fantastical instruments were sorely disappointed, however. "There is no more reason why my working on the elements should be done with effusions of smoke than there is why there must be something seen between the instruments of wireless telegraphy," Charles explained from the foot of the strange black tower he and Paul had erected.

Charles quickly developed an innate sense of how to work the press. He guarded the details of his formula closely, but he gave visiting reporters enough material to win them over.

"I will tell you what is inside, though," he told one visitor to Esperanza who had been prevented from climbing into the covered tower. "There are 104 galvanized iron evaporation pans, which contain the chemicals and some water used in my demonstrations." The reporter left convinced he had been witness to a wonder of the modern world.

The tower lay in the shadow of Mount Lowe, home to California's most famous observatory. At night its staff would check that all was well with Charles and Paul by throwing the beam of the observatory's huge searchlight on their camp. They'd signal back by waving their flashlights.

Mount Lowe's astronomer, Edgar Lucien Larkin, was a formidable figure, a polymath who had written books and newspaper articles not just on astronomy but the occult and other supernatural matters. He was inevitably drawn to the curious young rainmaker.

Soon Charles was climbing up the hill to the observatory for long chats. "[Larkin] saw him quite often. He was a great friend of Charles's," Paul recalled. "He was interested in astronomy and astrology and everything."

The rising popularity of astrology was a particular hobbyhorse of Larkin's. The stars were a matter for serious study, not the mumbo jumbo being printed in the syndicated horoscopes, he fumed in his own newspaper columns.

As he got to know Charles a little, however, he might have found himself pausing for a brief reassessment. Some of the qualities associated with Charles's birth sign—Cancer, a water symbol, naturally—chimed rather well with the quietly intense personality intriguing half the state of California. Cancerians supposedly had a powerful familial instinct and a strong streak of self-sufficiency. They also had a tendency toward introversion and secrecy. As the "winter siege" continued, the latter only added to the public's intrigue and unease.

Rain continued to fall in bursts during Christmas and in the runup to the New Year. It was a measure of the seriousness with which his operation was being taken that a panic then set in about the annual Tournament of Roses Parade, due to be held on

Monday, January 2. A poem appeared in several papers begging Charles to grant the city a dry day:

Oh Mister Hatfield, you've been good to us
You've made it rain in ways promiscuous!
From Saugus down to San Diego Bay
They bless you for the rains of yesterday.
But Mister Hatfield, listen now;
Make us this vow:
Oh, please, kind sir, don't let it rain Monday!

The parade organizers expressed their gratitude when rain fell in the morning but disappeared in time for the afternoon's events to pass off in sunshine.

By March, with his rain gauge showing 17.7 inches—just 0.3 inch short of his target—Charles was being congratulated by a new wave of visiting newsmen.

His fame had spread as far as San Francisco by now. When T. E. Murtaugh, a reporter from the *San Francisco Examiner*, arrived at Esperanza he clearly expected to meet a borderline madman. Instead he found himself falling for Charles's mesmerizing charm. "There is nothing about Hatfield to suggest the eccentric, the fanatic or the egotist. He bears not the ear-marks of genius, eccentricity in his countenance or in his dress. The student of human nature will find in his face a pair of sincere eyes that look you straight in the face, a rather sharp nose and a determined chin," Murtaugh wrote. Like so many before and after, Murtaugh was surprised by the rainmaker's office demeanor.

"In attire he was neatly clad in a gray business suit and spotless linen. One would not expect to find this neatness in the general camper or man of science," he wrote. "The first impressions of the character of the man were as favorable as the last."

He asked Charles to account for the vast area covered by the storm. "Surely your chemicals have not the power to attract at the circumference of an area of 11,000 miles square," he said.

THE SAN FRANCISCO EXAMINER

CHARLES M HATFIELD MAKES RAIN FALL AT WILL AND GAINS $1,000

SYSTEM EXPLAINED BY THE YOUNG WIZARD

Tells an "Examiner" Representative, First of All, How He Succeeded In Solving a Great Problem When Others Failed

WOOES NATURE, BUT THEY FOUGHT HER

"Favorable impressions." Hatfield hosts the *San Francisco Examiner*, March 19, 1905.

Charles evaded the question in his usual way. "Ah, that is something I cannot answer because it would involve the divulgence of my secret."

Murtaugh left the Wizard of Esperanza, as he dubbed Charles, impressed. "Censure and ridicule are the first tributes paid to scientific enlightenment by prejudiced ignorance," Charles told him at one point.

"Whatever censure and ridicule may be accorded the man hereafter, his present sincerity entitles him to the respect and consideration of those who scoff," Murtaugh concluded.

By April, Charles had collected his $1,000, and the city's newspaper columnists were struggling to form their conclusions about the miracle man.

Edward H. Hamilton of the *Los Angeles Examiner* wasn't sure whether Charles was from "the long line of rack-a-rock bombardiers of the skies who preceded him" or "merely a child of luck." Whatever he was, Hamilton—rightly—sensed that "the fellow, chemist or charlatan, scientist or fakir, is a figure about which speculation and inquiry might well love to linger."

Like many other newspapermen, Hamilton viewed Charles's emergence with a blend of snobbery, fascination, and faint dread.

"The suggestion that a man of this class should be given serious consideration is apt to provoke a pitying smile. But it is always to be remembered that the same pitying smile was wasted

47

on Stevenson, Fulton, Morse and the rest who did that which seemed to the men of their time impossible," he wrote. "There is always the haunting fancy that he really may be able to produce rain at will."

And if that were true, Hamilton concluded, expressing what must have been the darkest thought of many of his fellow citizens, what if Hatfield tapped into powers beyond his comprehension? What if he "produced a storm monster that he cannot control? He may be the Frankenstein of the air."

"PROFESSOR" HATFIELD

[Crow's Landing, 1905]

I n the wake of his success at Altadena, Charles's career took off like one of Clarence Jewell's rockets.

Such was his strange celebrity in Los Angeles in 1905 that people routinely used the word *Hatfielding* rather than *raining*. Enterprising merchants sold "Genuine 'Hatfield' Umbrellas" at up to $4.50 apiece. When hotel or restaurant managers saw Charles walking into their establishments, they would nod for their orchestras to strike up an apposite tune. "I'm on the Water Wagon" was his theme song in Pasadena. Wherever he went, crowds—often female—would huddle around, inveigling out of him a weather forecast or a promise not to rain on their corner of the city the following day.

The attention was gratifying, but Charles was more interested in being taken seriously. So he capitalized on the publicity by promoting himself as "Professor" Charles Hatfield. The first of a series of talks, titled "How I Attract Moisture Laden Atmosphere," took place at the Simpson Auditorium in Los Angeles in May 1905. It was a sellout.

By now Charles had distilled his ideas into a standard presentation that had already formed the basis of newspaper and magazine pieces under his byline.

His propaganda subtly tapped into the can-do spirit of the agrarian West:

We cannot force nature to do anything. But we can assist nature to do everything. Nature will respond willingly and freely to artificial assistance. Do we not fertilize and cultivate our ground to obtain better results? Yes. Do we not bud our orange trees to produce the Navel orange? Yes. Do we not hatch our chicks by artificial means? Yes. Do we not irrigate our vast stretches of desert waste by artificial canal systems? Yes. Does not Luther Burbank change fruits, flowers and plants to gigantic sizes? Yes. Then why not induce or assist nature to produce rainfall?

As well as the talk, Charles threw in a demonstration of his meteorological magnetism at work. "With clever little demonstrations of chemicals and test tubes, Hatfield showed how certain chemicals, combined and sent into the air from a funnel, would meet their affinity in the moisture and draw the dampness from all directions toward the desired spot," one impressed witness wrote. "A marvel of science, chemistry and the good common sense of a bright young man," he called the show.

Each demonstration brought a new flood of job offers.

In December, Charles and Paul arrived in the community of Crow's Landing, near Modesto, in the parched San Joaquin Valley north of Los Angeles. It was the second contract he'd been given

WIZARD OF ESPERANZA GIVES
FIRST LECTURE

PLEASES A LARGE AUDIENCE

By Clever Explanations and Numerous
Demonstrations He Shows How
It Is Possible to Draw Water
From Clouds

Charles M. Hatfield, chemist and
rainmaker, the only man in the world
who has made the uncertain occupation
of rainmaking a paying business, addressed a large number of enthusiastic
admirers last night at Simpson's auditorium on the subject, "How I Attract
Moisture Laden Atmosphere."
  The lecture was a marvel of science,
chemistry and the good common sense
of a bright young man.
  Hatfield succeeded famously with his
audience and those who attended went
away with the satisfied air that they
knew how rain was made.
  From the many expressions of the
people who entered the auditorium the
general impression seemed to be that
Hatfield had enticed rain from the
clouds by dressing as a medicine man
and dancing the "buffalo" on the Altadena hillsides.

"A Marvel of Science." Report on Hatfield's first "public performance," Simpson's
Auditorium, Los Angeles, May 1905.

in the area. The previous month he'd collected $750 after breaking a drought for the South Yuba Water Company nearby.

In Crow's Landing, however, he found a community in need of more than mere rain. The droughts had driven the farmers deep into debt. Many of them owed their landlord, Simon Newman, $1,500 and more. "Those farmers up there didn't even own the harness on their mules," Paul recalled later.

Charles cinched his contract with a public talk. His explanations of his method would have been difficult for the unschooled plowmen and cattle drovers to follow. They were difficult for anyone to understand. He would often speak in an excitable flurry of words, using his own lexicon of terms as if everyone knew what they meant. Yet the salesman in him had an innate sense of the message his audience wanted to hear. It could be summed up in one word: hope. By the end of his talk, he had convinced them he represented it.

Although Sigmund Freud may have been ushering in a new era of the self that year in Vienna, Charles—and the forces that now propelled him—needed no psychoanalysis. He had inherited many of his father's strong suits, not least a boundless entrepreneurial optimism. Like his father Charles always felt the biggest opportunity of his life was around the next corner. It was no blind optimism. Charles's enterprise, like his father's, was underpinned by his faith.

By his midtwenties, Charles had stopped attending Quaker meetings, but he retained what he called once "a deep reverence for religion." Elsewhere his dabbling would have been renounced as an insult to God; within Quakerism's tradition of dissent, individualism, and plainspokenness, however, such scientific freethinking sat comfortably. The movement even had a role model to inspire Charles. One of the first meteorological figures Charles would have come across was a Quaker, Luke Howard, the Englishman who in 1802 had come up with a classification for cloud types—cumulus, after the Latin for *heap*, for the lowest level clouds; cirrus, after the Latin for *lock of hair*, for the wispy, high-level formations; stratus for the dense, heavy-layered cloud types; and nimbus, for rain-bearing—that remained the standard used worldwide.

But there was something else driving Charles. He also felt empowered by the spirit of the age, the blend of ambition and confidence that had produced men like Henry Ford and, California's hero, the horticultural pioneer Luther Burbank. At the dawn of the new century, United States Senator Chauncey Depew had summed up the hyperconfidence of the era when he said that the average American felt "four hundred percent bigger" than the year before. It was a sense Charles already shared. At Crow's Landing, he learned he could deliver it to others as well.

He and Paul set to work erecting four towers. Soon each was belching out thick plumes of vapor. Within two weeks, a record 13.5 inches fell. In addition to a check for $1,000, he was immediately given a contract to work there between mid-November and mid-April the following winter.

The transformation of the region's mood was as remarkable as anything Charles and Paul had seen in the skies above them.

"The ranchers had big bills," Paul noted. "But they all paid him off."

"You may laugh if you like," one wheat farmer came to say, "but I figure that I have made $50,000 by Hatfield's operation."

News of his latest success was soon picked up by the Los Angeles newspapers. Once more they beat a path to his door.

In the wake of his first successes Charles had been an open and welcoming—if perplexing—interviewee. Reporters couldn't decide if he was "a genius, worthy to be placed with the inventor of X-rays, or merely a toy of Fortune, who, when she is tired of flirting, will trump him adrift to be the laughing stock of the nation." Each new journalist discovered like all those who came before and after that any attempt to winkle out his formula would be greeted with a well-practiced stonewalling act. "He fortifies it behind an impenetrable reticence. Whenever his interlocutor thinks he has framed a key question, a peculiar smile at the corner of Mr. Hatfield's mouth is followed by a draught in the conversation," one wrote.

It made him all the more appealing a character. One reporter found him "an attractive psychological study, almost as interesting in personality as the meteorological wonders that are credited to his wizardry skill."

In Washington, the chief of the U.S. Weather Bureau was certain what lay behind Charles's enigmatic silences.

Willis Moore's opinion of artificial rainmaking remained what it had been a decade earlier, when Dyrenforth was at work on his government's behalf. He didn't believe in it. At all. At first he had gagged George Franklin and the other Californian weath-ermen—even when the *Los Angeles Herald* had reduced Charles and Franklin to "rivals for the honor of bringing rain"—and billed it as a match: "Chemical Affinities v Science of the Forecaster."

In a letter to Moore, Franklin raged about Charles's method being based on "what would seem to be a new principle in physics." Moore told Franklin the only legal way to "check such imposters" was to ignore them, at least until they could be charged with obtaining money under false pretenses. As news-paper reports of Charles's success emerged from as far afield as Ohio, Moore was forced to act.

The report in the April edition of *Monthly Weather Review,* the bureau's official publication, was headlined FAKE RAINMAKING— A LETTER FROM THE CHIEF OF THE BUREAU and was a copy of the scathing letter he had sent the editor of the Ohio paper that had printed the piece, the *Toledo Blade.*

The *Blade* had run a piece on the Los Angeles rains in late March in which, according to Moore, it had implied they were "the result of a single rainmaking station on the slope of Mount Wilson." Moore countered: "Permit me to say that the liberation of chemicals on Mount Wilson had nothing to do with the rain-fall in southern California."

"Your dispatch stated that the heaviest rain fell in the region of the rainmaker, and that the rainfall had not been large in any of the other regions of the subarid West. This statement is erroneous, as during the same period general and excessive rains occurred throughout Arizona and New Mexico." Moore went on to ascribe the heavy rains to "general abnormal atmospheric conditions over the United States" and an "established" linkage between "low barometric pressure and excessive rains in the Southwest and high barometric pressure and unusual cold in the North and East." His argument was that because the winter had been excessively cold in the North and East, it was only natural that it had been extremely wet in the South and West.

Moore dismissed Charles's experiments as a waste of time and money. "The processes which operate to produce rain over large areas are of such magnitude that the effects upon them of the puny efforts of man are inappreciable."

Moore's broadside was picked up by three Los Angeles papers: the *Herald*, the *Examiner*, and the *Times*. WEATHER CHIEF RAPS HATFIELD ran the first's headline. HATFIELD EFFORT PUNY, SAYS CHIEF and RAIN AND HOT AIR ran the other two. But not everyone sided with the authorities.

The bureau chief found Charles had supporters—eloquent ones—many of whom harbored a pathological distrust of Washington. "Making rain has been practiced by savants in laboratories for half a century or more—of course on a small scale for the benefit of the students of chemistry, and Hatfield has simply done the same thing on a much larger scale, but under very much more favorable conditions," said one pro-Charles editorial.

"The wonder is that, like the wireless telegraphy, the secret has not been discovered and put into practical use scores of years sooner. There are more things in heaven and earth than are dreamed of in your philosophy, Mr. Moore."

PULLING THE PLUG

[Dawson City, June 1906]

On a broiling summer's day in June 1906, Charles and Paul looked out from the upper deck of the steamer *Selkirk* as it pulled up at the quayside of the self-styled capital of the Klondike, Dawson City. The image they saw would live with them for the rest of their days.

Below them a brass band played and the quayside was filled with a sea of onlookers decked out in oilskins and galoshes. Many were waving umbrellas. Paul later reckoned there were three thousand people in attendance, all of them asking the same question as they scanned the disembarking faces: "Where's the rainmaker? Where's the rainmaker?"

Despite the best efforts of the weather bureau, the boy wizard of Esperanza had by now been celebrated around the nation and the world. Across the Atlantic, in England, readers of the popular magazine *Tid-Bits* had in June 1905 pored over "A Chat with the World's Greatest 'Rain Maker.' " Charles assured his new English audience that he could succeed there, too. "No place or portion of the country is so unfavorable to the production of rain by artificial methods as Southern California, and the success I have met with there leads me to the belief that the same results might be obtained in any quarter of the globe." He was soon talking of a potential deal with the British government, although no record of it appears to exist.

It was left to the politicians of the frozen northwest of North America to become the first government to hire the rainmaking phenomenon. Charles had been approached by a Dawson City resident named Litchcox who had visited him at Eagle Rock late in 1905. Litchcox had offered Charles a contract to make rain the following June and July.

The news had sparked a national debate in Canada when it first seeped out. The country's chief astronomer, Otto J. Klotz, wrote to Willis Moore for advice. Moore, predictably, told him Charles was "a pretended rainmaker" of "considerable notoriety." Klotz went straight to the Canadian Parliament.

At a debate on the subject, the MP for Toronto, George E. Foster, wondered aloud at the potential consequences for the planet if they hired the controversial American. "Suppose that man Hatfield gets his apparatus at work and tinkers with the vast and delicate atmosphere of the universe, is it not possible that he may pull out a plug, or slip a cog, and this machinery of the universe once started going wrong may go on to the complete submersion of this continent."

However, Charles had his backers in the gold-rush country. Fred Rothschilds, the businessman who had seen the results of Charles's work in Los Angeles two years earlier, was among those who were vocal in their support. "Just tell the Dawson merchants to stock up on umbrellas, raincoats, rubber boots, and canoes. Dawson will need them when Hat pulls the plug," he said. "Klondike is to be congratulated on her rainmaking venture."

The contract Charles had agreed in principle with Litchcox went ahead.

Charles and Paul made the long journey north after finishing their latest contract with Crow's Landing in April. They sailed from Vancouver to Skagway on the *Princess Beatrice* in May, making their way to the Klondike via the Whitehorse Pass.

Rain was falling even as they began to set up a precipitation plant on King Solomon's Dome, twenty-five miles outside Dawson. "He has scared the heavens before starting," George Foster said.

Their arrival coincided with Paul's birthday, and they celebrated by sitting under the midnight sun eating wild strawberries.

As the steady drizzle and occasional hail fell, all seemed to be going Charles's way. A week or so after their arrival, a buggy carrying the president of the local Bank of Commerce arrived, flanked by a deputation of Mounted Police. "I want to show you something in the buggy, Hatfield," the banker announced.

"He pulled out a sack and there was fifty thousand dollars in nuggets," Paul remembered, years later. The gold represented two days' worth of "clean up" from a local creek. The haul was on its way down to Dawson and the bank.

The miners' gratitude was soon being reflected in the papers. One poem read:

> *Ye gods of snow, of storm and shower,*
> *Behind what Hatfield doth this hour,*
> *His 'lectro chemical vapors rise,*
> *To wet the world and ease the skies.*

Within days, however, the summer heat had returned, warming the political climate once more. The rains may have been enough for the placer miners but to those who mined hydraulically they were far from satisfactory. They were soon making their impatience

BELIEVES IN HAT
—

F. Rothschilds Knows
From Trial

ORDER UMBRELLAS
——

"Certainly I believe in rainmakers,"
said Fred Rothschilds, manager of the
Canadian-Klondike company, as he
leaned back in the chair in the Regina
lobby and congratulated Tom Bruce
on his trust-made Africana.
"Why, yes; rainmakers are a blessing.

Wizard of the North. The Klondike welcomes Hatfield. *Dawson Weekly News*, Friday,
April 13, 1906.

known through the Dawson papers. Charles defended himself and
claimed he was fighting conditions that reminded him of a desert.
His hygrometer showed 30 percent humidity when he arrived.
"The relative humidity today is from 60 to 85 per cent, so you will
see that we have broken the drought," he told the *Yukon World*.

But he was soon spending most of his time at the foot of the
tower in meetings with miners and their agents. Matters came to
a head at the end of the month. Weather bureau criticism had
found its way to some of the more disgruntled miners. Many
were already bridling at the prospect of the $10,000 payout
Charles would be due if his trip was deemed a success. Charles
was soon dismantling the tower and preparing for the return
steamer trips to Skagway, Vancouver, and then home. He left
with $1,100 in expenses.

Charles was not so naïve as to expect everyone to believe in
him. He understood the way he divided opinion and, publicly at
least, had come to an accommodation with that fact. "It is a well

known fact that censure and ridicule are the first tributes to scientific enlightenment by prejudiced ignorance," he would say, adopting the high ground. "Take the greatest inventors of ancient or modern times, like Galileo and Morse. Their views were laughed at and yet they laid the foundations of some of our greatest scientific works."

Yet his sense of fair play was always offended by those who questioned his honesty. He complained once that he had received "some of the hardest 'knocking' a man ever suffered. Letters have been written . . . to the effect that I am a fakir [sic], a grafter and several other things."

The very public ending of his Klondike contract was the biggest knock yet. The voyage south back to Vancouver and Southern California was a long and uncomfortable one. Although his faith in his own abilities remained unbroken, he couldn't fail to recognize the damage the bad publicity had caused him. He would deny it to the press, of course. But inwardly, doubts must have taken form for the first time in his career. Was his great opportunity no longer ahead of him? Had he left it back in the nightless land now receding into the horizon?

"A DIRE NECESSITY"

[Eagle Rock, Spring 1913]

I n the wake of the Klondike trip, doubts began to hit him harder. They were bound to. Hatfield's priorities and his life were changing. New, more practical pressures were soon heaped upon him.

Charles's easygoing charm had always made him popular with women, even when he was just a plain sewing-machine salesman. His continuing celebrity around Los Angeles, Pasadena, and San Diego made him even more of an attraction. Society women would crowd around him in public, giddily asking whether they should cancel their afternoon tea parties or go shopping with their parasols in case of rain. Charles remained shy at heart and found their naïveté hard to take. "Hatfield was plainly embarrassed by the questions the ladies asked him," recorded a witness who once saw "a little crowd of interrogators" swirl around him in a Pasadena hotel lobby. Eventually he couldn't help but respond to the attention.

In San Diego he met and fell in love with Mable Rulon. Six years Charles's junior, she had come to California to put the past behind her. Her marriage to Lawrence Wright, an Iowa dentist, had ended in divorce. She headed west with her two young children, Leila and Richard, to be reunited with her family, who had settled in San Diego. When she met Charles, she was living with her father Jesse, a successful engineer, and her mother Mary Jane, known to everyone as Jennie. The family lived in a big town house in the prosperous suburb of University Heights.

To Charles, the warmth with which Mable's family welcomed him was as beguiling as his sweetheart. Mable's mother was a feisty customer and an unashamed admirer of the region's famous rainmaker. She was defending him against the sneers mere days after her daughter introduced him to the family. When Paul started seeing Mable's younger sister, Edna, the familial ties became tighter still. The foursome became inseparable. Soon both Rulon girls married the Hatfield brothers and moved north, to Pasadena.

With Richard and Leila, Charles and Mable settled in a single-story bungalow at 208 Royal Drive in Eagle Rock. Paul and Edna set up their home nearby. The financial pressures on Paul quickly hardened with the birth of a son, Robert.

When there were no rainmaking contracts, Paul rolled up his sleeves and took whatever work was going. "Anything, anything." Charles was not prepared to face that option yet.

To the farmers of the southwest Charles remained a beacon of hope. At Crow's Landing in particular, people's faith had, if anything, deepened. It was there that he recovered his confidence in the wake of the Klondike setback. After two weeks of work in 1907, he had beaten his target of 12 inches by a margin of 2 inches. The rain fell so hard at one point that a group of farmers visited the camp and begged Charles and Paul to pack up and head home. "They came out and told us: 'Gee, we can't even plow, you fellows get out and get going,' " Paul recalled. "They paid us off and away we went." By 1911, he had worked seven successful seasons in the San Joaquin Valley.

Testimonials from the area found their way to farming communities near and far. Close to home he was popular in the town of Hemet, not far from Pasadena, where he had first been contracted to deliver 4 inches in 1907. He beat the target by 3 inches. He was still working there in 1912 when he scored a $4,000 contract to fill the lake of the Hemet Land and Water Company. Farther afield, he had new admirers in Oregon and Texas. In the Texan town of Carlsbad, where he was hired by the San Angelo Chamber of Commerce, Charles put up three huge towers and delivered rain above the average for the region. In Sherman County, Oregon, the arrival of his towers signaled the beginning of a dousing that produced almost four times the normal 0.62 inches. In March 1911, that success won him a contract with farmers in the nearby community of Patterson. Ordinarily, the local stream, the Orestimba, was "a depression in the landscape which is a little dryer than the surrounding fields." That month heavy rains swelled the river to a width of half a mile. Cellars in Patterson were flooded for the first time in living memory, and such was the overflow from the Orestimba that a canal ran uphill. Charles left with a contract to return the following year.

Yet for all the small-town success Charles was winning, there was a sense that he had lost the momentum of the early years. It was easy to isolate the cause. Willis Moore and his campaign of writing to newspaper editors had slowly begun to damage him. As a result several potential clients had decided, as Charles delicately put it, "they do not care to have dealings with a person such as my enemies are endeavoring to make me out."

Some setbacks stung worse than others. He cited an offer from a big cattle-raising company in Kansas who had made "a liberal offer of straight salary and additional cash rewards." "I accepted it and the news reached the papers. Suddenly the company's correspondence ceased. I am not to receive one penny for my efforts."

He could not be so measured about a loss he suffered in early 1913. In his still-regular chats with the newspapers, Charles continued to talk up the prospects of lucrative foreign contracts. His grander ambitions included ridding London of its notorious "pea soup" fogs and irrigating the Sahara. Of the latter prospect he enthusiastically—and probably quite seriously—admitted: "I should like to have the contract for watering the desert of the Sahara as soon as the French Government can be made to appreciate that I can really make as much rain as my employers order." These were not empty boasts. In October 1912 he became involved in negotiations with the government of South Africa. For a fee of $10,000—and the cost of transporting himself, Paul, and their equipment from California—he promised to break a drought in Karoo, on the Western Cape. Once more Charles became the subject of a parliamentary inquiry. This time the chief meteorologist of the Irrigation Department of Pretoria wrote to Washington intrigued by the "remarkable statements" made by Hatfield.

In the spring of 1913, the inquiry landed on the desk of Willis Moore, whose response was predictably damning. He condemned Charles for "practicing deception" and making "a dire necessity the occasion for the perpetrating of a fraud."

As the year wore on, Charles waited in vain for a reply from Africa. It never came.

"HEADS WE WIN, TAILS HE LOSES"

[San Diego, Winter 1915]

heir paths were always destined to cross. Like Charles Hatfield, San Diego believed itself on the brink of greatness. Like him, the city believed it could mold nature to achieve it. The Western Union telegram that arrived at Charles's home at Eagle Rock on the afternoon of December 8, 1915, merely confirmed the inevitable. It read:

IN MATTER OF PRECIPITATION PLANT AT MORENA CAN YOU BE PRESENT WITH COMMON COUNCIL TOMORROW AFTER-NOON IF NOT STATE WHEN YOU CAN BE HERE

Allen H. Wright, San Diego City Council

It had taken Charles's new "agent," Fred Binney, to make the match.

65

Charles always prided himself on his honesty and plain-dealing nature. Neither were qualities many associated with Binney. Simply put, he was the kind of man who gave rainmaking a bad name.

An Englishman with a voice as highly pitched as his opinion of himself, Binney's interest in rainmaking was borne of personal misfortune. The droughts of the late 1890s had wiped out the citrus groves he owned in the town of Helix. He corresponded with—and possibly hired—Clayton Jewell. He certainly claimed to have known Jewell well enough to correct the *San Diego Union* when it printed the Rock Island rainmaker's secret in 1900. It was "five pounds, not five ounces of zinc that was required," he volunteered. Binney also suggested that the hydrogen method be tried in San Diego for thirty days at four stations to be placed at Otay, Lemon Grove, Linda Vista, and Oceanside. Unsurprisingly, the city council chose to ignore him.

No one doubted his energy. Binney was a heroic walker and thought nothing of marching the fifteen miles from San Diego to the coast at La Jolla. Also undisputed was his evangelical belief in rainmaking. Binney had written lengthy, loquacious arguments in favor of methods from the sulphuric acid and zinc fume-raising of Jewell to a scheme for using liquid air to cool the atmosphere. It was his trustworthiness that was at issue.

Among local realtors he was known for painting his own FOR SALE signs and taking liberties where he placed them. The proper-ties he advertised were generally "pretty homes with nice gardens and pretty flowers," but didn't always turn out that way. An Eng-lishman named Alonzo de Jessop immigrated to California, only to discover Binney had sold the San Francisco ranch he thought was his to someone else. The Jessops realized that their mistake had been to take Binney's word as his bond. "In England when you give your word that you're going to do something, you don't have to write it down—that's it," de Jessop reflected ruefully.

In an age when newspapers treated almost all the information it received with naïve acceptance, Binney's frequent contributions on rainmaking and other matters were taken with healthy pinches of salt.

When reports on his latest pronouncements were published, they generally appeared under the cautionary headline: AS F. A. BINNEY SEES IT.

However, no one could accuse Binney of a lack of persistence. He had known Charles's family for years and had followed his career closely. Some even suspected Binney of giving Charles his early rain-stew recipe. Whatever the truth, by 1913 the Englishman correctly sensed a waning in the fortunes of the great rainmaking wonder of the world.

Fred Binney began working on Charles's behalf even before the South Africa rejection. His first attempt to persuade San Diego to hire his client, in 1912, had come to naught. Binney did not take it well when the Wide Awake Improvement Society, a local boosters' group, had turned down the offer. "There are all sorts of wonders you believe in, like wireless and Burbank's new plants and automobiles. But when a man comes in with a simple sensible idea, you treat him as though he were a lunatic," Binney protested. But by the winter of 1915, he knew the climate had changed dramatically.

The previous year, the city had agreed to pay $4 million to acquire ownership of the Southern California Mountain Water Company, San Diego's biggest privately owned utility. The necklace of dams, flumes, and connecting conduits stretched sixty miles southeast into the mountainous backcountry. The deal meant that for the first time in its history, the city owned a system capable, at least in theory, of meeting its growing water demands. But some wondered if it had actually acquired a white elephant.

The sale of the SCMWC confirmed two things: Water was still San Diego's Achilles' heel, and the duo of Elisha Babcock and John Spreckels were the city's preeminent business force.

Babcock, a wealthy civil engineer from Evanston, Illinois, was thirty-four years old when, in 1884, his doctor sent him to California to recover from tuberculosis. He wasted no time in growing his fortune, paying $110,000 for just over 4,000 acres of undeveloped oceanfront land in San Diego. There he built the city's grandest hotel, the Hotel del Coronado, a cross between a Norman castle and a fairy palace that boasted 399 bedrooms and a theater and ballroom that covered 111,000 square feet. With the area transformed, Babcock sold the adjoining land for $2 million.

His partner in the hotel development was John Spreckels, the son of San Francisco "Sugar King" Claus Spreckels. Spreckels's other investments included the *San Diego Union* and the so-called "impossible railway" connecting San Diego with Yuma, Arizona, across the desert and through granite mountain gorges. Both men saw money in San Diego's most precious commodity.

The solutions the city had found for its perennial water problems had become as audacious as they were ambitious. The first of the city's great water barons, Theodore S. Van Dyke, had been hunting in the Cuyamaca Mountains when he saw what the backcountry residents had known for generations: that at a certain altitude, the mountains cradled large bodies of settled water. Van Dyke returned to the city and set his sights on building a dam that would be connected to the city by a fifty-mile-long flume.

The city laughed at him, so he went to London and found plenty of wealthy Englishmen willing to take a flier on his wild idea. The dam was completed in 1886. But it was the flume that captured the imagination. Built almost entirely of redwood on a pine base, it used up 9 million feet of lumber. It was 35.6 miles long and supported in places by trestles teetering 80 feet above the ground. It was a feat of engineering and ingenuity worthy of discussion in *Scientific American*, although even its earnest reporter missed the story when the flume was officially opened with 125-foot-tall fountains, boosterish speeches, and a mile-long parade on February 22, 1889. Citizens tasted the new water and rejoiced at the improvement. What they did not know was that the Cuyamaca water had got stuck in the pipes miles away from the new town on the day of the celebrations. Van Dyke and his officials couldn't face missing their grand opening and quietly substituted the old salty stuff, pumped in for the day from Mission Valley.

His nerve had infected Babcock and Spreckels, who by now had formed the SCMWC. Babcock personally oversaw their initial project, a dam along the Otay River, completed in 1894. Until then dams had been of two types: masonry or hydraulic fill (a method used at Cuyamaca, among others, in which hydraulically pumped water was used to drive gravel and rock rubble into position to form a dam wall). Despite his lack of formal training as a water engineer, Babcock came up with a design of his own.

He first formed a large barrier by riveting together sections of steel plate that were 0.3 inch thick. This was lined with burlap, anchored to a masonry foundation, then encased in concrete. Finally rock and gravel fill were placed on both sides of the dam in the usual way. The Lower Otay Dam was finished in August 1897.

Soon afterward, the company completed a second dam farther up the river, the Upper Otay Dam. Here too Babcock courted controversy—the dam was only 14 feet wide at its base, tapering up to 4 feet in thickness at its top.

The final piece in the jigsaw was the most ambitious dam of all, high in the mountains at Morena. In addition to the dam, Babcock and Spreckels set to work on a scheme even more ambitious than Van Dyke's flume. The plan was to link Morena to the city—and so with the Otay system below. Over the next ten years, 13 miles of concrete conduits were built to carry the water. Miners drilled 9,000 feet of six-foot-wide tunnel through the granite and porphyry mountainsides at a cost of $20 per foot. In all, the scheme cost $450,000, but it soon turned a handsome profit.

In 1912, Spreckels offered to sell the SCMWC to the city for $4 million. The deal was controversial, but, using his newspapers to promote the cause, Spreckels clinched the sale two years later. The city raised the money through a bond offering.

Unfortunately, the acquisition of the system coincided with a rainless spell that stirred memories of the terrible seven-year drought of the 1890s. By December 1915, according to the city's attorney, Shelley Higgins, the city's supply of water had "dwindled alarmingly." The Lower Otay Reservoir was as "shallow as a pane of glass." But Morena was the greatest source of frustration. In theory the dam was capable of holding fifteen billion gallons of water; yet, since construction was finished in 1912 Morena had never been remotely near full. Higgins confided that the city was "frantic" to fill the mile-high monolith. So when Fred Binney approached the city council again, he found a caucus of councilmen close to desperation. They agreed to talk to Charles. All he had to do was persuade them.

On December 11, 1915, Charles marched into City Hall, starched and pressed, a model of quiet self-assurance. His future hinged on the next hour or so, but to look at him he might just as easily have been climbing a suburban porch to sell a housewife a Singer sewing machine.

Charles's sense of his own image was clear from the few photographs he allowed to be taken of himself at work. He dressed like a salesman and maintained what one visitor to his rainmaking tower called a "neatness one would not expect to find in a man of science." Even during the hard hauling labor at the tower, he wore the uniform of the professional man: pinstripes, white collar, tie, felt fedora. His favored pose for photographers, of him skillfully balancing flasks of chemicals in one hand while dispensing his secret formula with the other, underlined the message: he was an artisan, not a scam artist; a scientist, not an illusionist.

His polished air caught the councilmen by surprise. The meeting was attended by the nonvoting mayor, Edward Capps, and five councilmen; Herbert Fay, Walter Moore, Percy Benbough, Henry Manney, and Otto Schmidt. The city's manager, Fred Lockwood, and two members of the legal department, the city's attorney Terence Cosgrove and his deputy Shelley Higgins, were also in the chamber.

Men like Fay and Moore had memories of the city's previous flirtations with rainmakers. But Hatfield was clearly no Jewell or Dyrenforth. Shelley Higgins observed that the rainmaker "bore himself importantly and had what salesmen term impressive presence."

In dealing with farmers, Charles had learned to keep his contracts short and sweet. The farmers of Hemet, California, had signed an agreement that stretched to just a dozen words: "Four Inches of Rain for Four Thousand Dollars. No Rain. No Pay." But experience had also taught Hatfield to offer his customers a choice when necessary. He used the meeting to lay out three options.

The first had formed the basis of the original letter he sent the council, accepting their invitation to a meeting. It stipulated that he would provide 40 inches of rain "free gratis" between January 1 and June 1, 1916—but he would be paid $1,000 per inch for every inch between 40 and 50. "For all rainfall above 50 inches, no charges whatever to be asked." This offer had been submitted with a picture of a lake in Stanislaus County, north of San Diego, which Charles claimed had "overflowed for the first time in its history" soon after he erected his rainmaking towers nearby.

The offer and picture were filed on December 8. Now, three days later, Charles added two alternative options. The first was the simplest: "To fill the Morena Reservoir to overflowing between now and next December 20, 1916, for the sum of $10,000." The second was to deliver "30 inches of rain free of charge, you to pay me $500 per inch from the 30th to 50th inch, all above 50 inches to be free, on or before June 1st, 1916."

As the meeting progressed, it was clear that the council was leaning toward the most straightforward proposal: $10,000 to fill Morena within a year. In advance of the meeting, Fred Lockwood, the city's manager, had been asked to check the state of Morena's water supply. The water department reported back on December 10 that Morena contained "approximately 5 billion gallons" of water, about one-third of its capacity. In effect, Hatfield would be paid $10,000 for delivering 10 billion gallons of water. Some committee members could remember the city's pleasure at signing a deal with John Spreckels in October 1905, in which the water baron offered 7.776 million gallons a day for ten years—for $0.04 per 1,000 gallons. That was the cheapest water anywhere in California. Charles was offering water at one-fortieth of that price: $0.001 cent per 1,000 gallons. "It's heads we win, tails he loses," someone said. A motion to proceed along these lines was proposed.

With a show of hands, the motion was passed by a majority of four to one. Councilmen Moore, Benbough, Manney, and Schmidt raised their arms in favor. Only Herbert Fay registered a vote against. He thought the whole thing amounted to "rank foolishness."

PART II

"The Art of Hocus Pocus"
[January 1–9, 1916]

Fifth Avenue, San Diego, looking north from E Street. (San Diego Historical Society)

THE CAMP

[Morena, Saturday, January 1, 1916]

From a distance, the camp that had taken shape on a ridge on the northern slopes above Lake Morena resembled a small military outpost. Two large white munitions tents caught the eye first, their canopies reflecting in the morning sun and a thin plume of steam rising from the small stovepipe in one of them. A few yards away stood the skeleton of an observation tower. At the other side of the camp a flagpole supported a starched Old Glory. Occasionally a fedora-topped figure would complete the scene, slowly pacing the perimeter fence, drawing on a cheroot and cradling a rifle as he went. Except for the odd gopher or rabbit, there was little at which to aim the gun.

Charles had always prided himself on the militaristic precision with which he ran his operation. With Paul, he quickly slipped back into the soldierly routine.

In its design, location, and layout, the camp was a distillation of the lessons of a dozen years' rainmaking. Charles's method demanded large volumes of water, so he had chosen a spot that was elevated yet within easy reach of the reservoir. It also gave him a clear 360-degree view of the mountain skies—and a view of the road up from the dam. Close to a cluster of cottonwoods, it also provided shelter from the wind and shade from the broiling mountain sun.

Inside the camp's perimeter, the two tents—always referred to as tent A and tent B—stood side by side. The A tent served as Charles's and Paul's office, sleeping quarters, and general center of operations; the B tent served as storage for their food, cooking stove, and chemical supplies. Inside the cramped A tent, emptied boxes and spare timber were used as chairs and the desk at which Charles kept his daily log. To Charles—and his visitors—the order of the place was a symbol of his rigor and application. "Its tidy appearance distinctly showed that its occupant was devoted to neatness and method," one of the few reporters allowed in wrote of Charles's inner sanctum.

Subtler touches told the stories of past misfortunes. An army of enormous Texas ants had once burrowed into the A tent, infesting everything; now both tents were sealed and built on a foundation of wooden floorboards. Earlier in their career, at Hemet, California, Charles and Paul had returned from a brief outing to discover that opossums had eaten the supply of bacon they left hanging from the B tent's ridgepole; now their larder was kept under lock and key.

Unwelcome visitors were a constant concern. Charles threaded a string of small sleigh bells, sensitive to the slightest vibration, on to the wire fence that marked the perimeter of their camp. In case of more serious incursions, he also kept a rifle, pistol, or bowie knife close at hand. "I have a small arsenal inside the tent and I can assure you that anyone that is looking for trouble will find it," Charles told one arrival at his camp.

Charles and Paul raised their "precipitation plant" on New

Year's Eve. It was a simple tower, 14 square feet at the base, tapering up to 12 square feet at the top. Charles and Paul put it together in sections on the ground, then hauled it upright. A platform, with a small hole to aid circulation, was placed on top. A sea of cast-iron pans were then set out for the chemicals. Tar paper—another security measure—was wrapped around the working area.

The tower's basic design was unchanged since the brothers' earliest experiments. For a brief period, Charles had tried a metallic smokestack designed to condense and direct the vapor column. It proved cumbersome and prone to overheating and was discarded with no discernible damage to his rainmaking record. "It didn't do any good," said Paul.

The only real variable was the height of the tower. In areas where visits from "curiosity seekers" were likely, Charles often put the platform up to thirty feet in the air. In more isolated spots the tower could be lower. At Morena they felt safe placing the platform a dozen or so feet above the ground.

In the past few weeks, people all over San Diego had buttonholed Charles with stories about Morena's lack of rain. He heard how rain clouds piled up over the mountain reservoir but then drifted on without emptying; instead the rain fell on the eastern slopes of the Laguna range, toward the Salton Sea desert and Arizona. Charles was immune to such stories by now. Everyone was a weather expert, especially in his company. He generally ignored them and stuck to what he knew.

By the time the sun appeared over the horizon that morning, Charles and Paul were at work. Paul had observed his brother at work a dozen times and more over the years. This week there was a purpose to his movements that was unusual, Paul recalled years later. He sensed it from the moment Charles produced the keys that would unlock the chest containing the chemicals. Charles always guarded the box with the mistrust of a medieval alchemist, but he'd been more guarded than ever in San Diego and on the way up to Morena. Paul saw that instead of the normal casket of chemicals, Charles had packed two.

"I'm going to give them the works," he told Paul.

Draining his coffee, he disappeared up the ladder and behind the tar-paper wall of the tower. Within minutes Paul tasted the first acrid wave of chemical fumes in his nostrils. Above the tower, he saw the column of heated air, refracted and shimmering against the backdrop of the trees. Higher still, he knew the first faint plumes of vapor were curling their way into the atmosphere.

INCANTATIONS

[San Diego, Sunday, January 2, 1916]

The weekend edition of the *San Diego Union* arrived on the city's doorsteps with a dull thump. The paper contained the usual roundup of local, national, and international news, small ads and sporting tidbits. But its substance today was dramatized by a long supplement devoted to the boosterish braggings of the Exposition.

No trick of salesmanship was missed. Under headlines such as WONDER COUNTRY RICH IN VIRGIN RESOURCES and OCEAN-SIDE BLESSED WITH MANIFOLD ADVANTAGES, the *Union's* writers had penned verbose paeans to every corner of the county. A story on the southern suburb of Chula Vista ("beautiful view" in Spanish) revealed that one-eighth of America's lemons were now grown there. Accompanying it was a piece headlined: FAMOUS

SCIENTIST PROCLAIMS LEMONS AS MOST WHOLESOME OF FRUITS GROWN IN THE WORLD.

Even the city's less-reputable attractions were boosted. Plenty of people thought the new racetrack about to open, just across the Mexican border at Tijuana, an abomination. The *Union* celebrated its opening. SAN DIEGO'S FIFTEEN YEAR DREAM REALIZED WHEN COURSE AT BORDER TOWN BECOMES REALITY, ran the headline.

The city's burgeoning movie industry was also touted. In a literal sense, the California film industry had actually begun in San Diego when the Edison Company shot scenes of a double-decker trolley and the downtown district in 1891. Now a group of filmmakers had returned to Southern California to escape the illegal bullying of the Motion Pictures Patents Company, a cartel led by Edison. At La Mesa, Allan Dwan's Flying A Studios shot westerns and documentaries. In Coronado, Sigmund Lubin's Coronado Company was making short dramas "filmed entirely in San Diego." At his new studio in the southern suburb of National City, M. B. Dudley was filming a series of stories from the *Saturday Evening Post*.

Dudley, for one, was convinced the border city might end up overtaking Los Angeles as the focus of the embryonic West Coast industry. "I doubt if in the entire world there is a section so thoroughly and admirably adapted to the taking of motion pictures as that in the immediate vicinity of San Diego," he said.

For those without the patience to plow through every word of the *Union's* epic encomium to the city, there was a neat summary of the highlights. Soon it would look like an exercise in bleak irony. But for now it consisted of a roll call of the city's strongest selling points beneath the banner: WHY SAN DIEGO EXCELS. The fifty or so bullet-pointed attractions included:

- The most nearly perfect climate in the United States, with warm winters, cool summers, and almost perpetual sunshine.
- The San Diego and Arizona Railway, nearly completed.

• A city-owned water system, the largest of its kind in California, outside the aqueduct system of Los Angeles.

Dissent was not one of the *Union's* strong suits, particularly when it came to the Exposition and the promotion of San Diego. The paper was owned by John Spreckels, who never hesitated to use it for his own political ends. So it was little surprise that no one wondered why, if San Diego's climate and water system were so perfect, the city's councilmen had turned to a rainmaker to fill their biggest reservoir.

In truth, since his hiring in mid-December, Charles had been all but forgotten. His deal with the city had been front-page news— briefly. Reporting the council's decision to send him to Morena, the *San Diego Union* echoed the "heads we win, tails he loses" sentiment of the mayor's chamber. "If Hatfield makes his promise good the city will secure about ten billion gallons of water at an average cost of one-tenth of a cent per thousand gallons. If the 'rainmaker' fails to keep his word 'to fill Morena to overflowing,' the city will be under no obligation to pay him anything."

"Go right ahead, Charles Hatfield, and make it rain," said a piece in the *San Diego Sun.*

Only the *Union's* Sunday columnist, Yorick, had given the matter any serious consideration. His attitude typified the blend of "what do we have to lose?" levity and mild condescension with which the city seemed to regard the whole enterprise.

Yorick wasn't willing to dismiss Charles out of hand. "I am not inclined to deprecate the action of our City in bargaining with Rainmaker Hatfield for a wet winter," he wrote in a long piece on December 19. "My skepticism as to the ultimate deluge is quite as obstinate as that of many of my fellow citizens, but I cannot forget that the scoffers who derided Rainmaker Noah in somewhat similar circumstances paid a severe and permanent penalty for their unbelief."

Like many around the city, Yorick was impressed by Charles's straightforward nature. "It is creditable to the honesty of Rainmaker

Rainmaker' Gets Contract
From City to Fill Morena
Reservoir for $10,000

Heads We Win, Tails He
Loses,' Agreement Termed
"Foolishness."

"HEADS, we win; tails, he loses": contract was authorized yesterday by the Council between the the City Council between and Charles M. Hatfield, the "rainmaker," when the moisture accelerator promised to fill Morena reservoir to overflowing by December 20, 1916, for the sum of $10,000.

All the councilmen voted in favor of the contract, except Fay, who termed it "rank foolishness."

"Rank Foolishness." The *San Diego Union* reports the hiring of Hatfield, December 14, 1915.

Hatfield's intention that he does not pretend ability to make it rain when there is no rain in sight." He couldn't resist suggesting the hiring was something of a joke, however. "If Rainmaker Hatfield can make enough rain to fill the Morena dam he will receive $10,000: if he doesn't he gets nothing. In my opinion it is an excellent business proposition from the city's standpoint. The publicity alone is worth more than $10,000."

The arrival of the first eyewitnesses back from Morena only added to the faintly mocking air surrounding the enterprise. If the Hatfield contract was to be taken seriously, it was only for the purpose of poking serious fun.

Shelley Higgins, the city's deputy attorney, claimed to have seen puffs of smoke and heard explosions as he drove through the nearby mountains in his hired Model T. "It was Hatfield, shooting bombs, exploding them in an incantation aimed at wringing moisture from the air," he recalled later.

H. F. Kirkwood, the city employee who had driven Charles and Paul to the reservoir, arrived back in town with stories of his own. Although he had left Morena while the Hatfield brothers were still erecting their tower, he couldn't resist the temptation to embellish. He was soon spinning a tale about the strange ritual he had witnessed on his way down the mountain. High above him, astride the rainmaking tower, Kirkwood had seen Hatfield "waving his arms on the north edge of the platform, then on the south and the east and west edges mumbling the art of hocus pocus."

PECULIAR

[Morena, Monday, January 3, 1916]

Three days into the new year, Seth Swenson and his wife Maggie were already growing uneasy about their new neighbors.

Swenson knew the rarefied terrain around the dam and its reservoir better than any man alive. It was now a decade since he had first arrived in the mountains. He had been at the helm of a mule train that had hauled a steam boiler belonging to the SCMWC up the twisting mountain passes. Back then Morena was a lush landscape of dense woodland and steep gorges. The main river, the Cottonwood, was fed by the crystal waters of three creeks, Kitchen, La Posta, and Mahagaut. In winter, melted snow and runoff rain swelled the creeks and turned the Cottonwood into a torrent. Through the long construction of the dam,

Seth had operated the boiler. When the 150-foot wall was completed in 1912, he had jumped at the chance to become Morena's first damkeeper.

Until now his routine had been confined to maintaining the dam's outlet towers and spillways and performing a regular check of the reservoir's water gauge. It wasn't the most demanding job in the world; occasionally he would find time to help fishermen pinpoint the best spots to fish for bluegill, crappie, catfish, or bass.

Charles's arrival had made life busier. The Swensons were to act as the rainmaker's link with the city. Since the brothers' arrival before New Year's Eve, Seth and Maggie had relayed messages back and forth to the tower most days. With the rainmaker at work, Seth was also expected to phone in a daily 7:00 A.M. gauge reading to the water impoundment office at San Diego City Hall. The gauge's markings went up to just over 150 feet. On January 3 he had recorded the water level at 118.71 feet. That translated to a storage figure of 5.195 billion gallons. Two million gallons of runoff had arrived in the past twenty-four hours. It was good news, but not enough to lift his unease.

The Hatfield brothers had set up camp a mile or so from the damkeeper's cottage, but even at that distance the chemical stench was overpowering. One visitor once wondered whether "a limberger [sic] cheese factory had broken loose. These gases smell so bad it rains in self-defense."

At first the Swensons saw nothing odd in the way that whenever they approached the camp, the two strangers set down their tools and quickstepped across the perimeter fence to intercept them. It was only later that the penny dropped: the brothers were guarding the details of their method and the secret formula.

"As if I would know anything about it," Maggie muttered to herself.

The Swensons were not the first people to find Charles a friendly and talkative—if puzzling—character. He had little patience for small talk, preferring instead to cut straight to a discussion of the latest gauge reading or weather forecast from the city. He also had a habit of launching into long and elliptical talks about the science of rainmaking. Seth tried his best to follow, but he would invariably walk away shaking his head. "He'd talk non-stop for fifteen minutes then you'd go off wondering what he said."

Maggie found Charles's soliloquies equally alienating. Sometimes she suspected his persona was perhaps his greatest invention of all. "You never really knew the man," she said later. "There was something sort of mysterious—sort of peculiar—about him. I often had the feeling that I was talking to someone who was wearing a mask."

Yet on other occasions he struck Maggie as the most self-possessed man she had ever encountered. The conversation she'd had with him on that Monday morning was a perfect example. After baffling her with another convoluted explanation of his method, Charles said, "I'm a scientist, not a magician," and went on to promise rain was on its way.

"When will this happen?" Maggie asked.

It wasn't his answer so much as the certainty with which he delivered it that had been playing on her mind ever since.

"In a few days," Charles said.

HARD WORK

[Morena, Tuesday, January 4, 1916]

Charles's scarecrow appearance belied his capacity for hard work.

He always took the lion's share of the duties up on the tower, regularly putting in seventeen-hour days. He would work the graveyard shift, until 4:00 A.M., grab four hours' sleep in his cot, then take over again at 8:00 A.M. He worked through the day, took a three-hour nap between 5:00 P.M. and 8:00 P.M., and started all over again.

For the past two days, however, the workload had seemed more onerous than ever. The rains of New Year's Eve had been fleeting. When the winds dropped, the temperature had nudged the mercury into the high 90s. Away from the tower, the mountain air was dry and scented with pine and cottonwood, acacia and eucalyptus, but also heat and dust. The intensity of it caught Paul off guard. By the afternoon of Sunday, January 2, he had begun to feel dizzy. That evening he collapsed with what he guessed later was "heat prostration." Charles rolled up his sleeves and took on his brother's duties in addition to his own. He also played the roles of nursemaid and counselor to his dispirited younger brother.

The skies had been mostly clear until now, with only the prairie falcons wheeling overhead to break the blue monotony. But Charles remained confident. He let loose a new batch of chemicals that morning. By early afternoon, the temperature had dropped and clouds were moving in. Paul was in the A tent when the sound of rain on canvas roused him from his sleep.

"RAIN PUSHER"

[San Diego, Wednesday, January 5, 1916]

T he headline of the next morning's *San Diego Union* read: RAIN
AT MORENA; DID HATFIELD MILK SKIES?

"There was rain at Morena yesterday," the brief report
began, "but whether it was due to what is described in the law
books as an 'act of God' or to the efforts of Charles Hatfield,
the 'rain pusher' who is striving to win $10,000 from the city by
filling Morena reservoir with water, is a subject upon which even
the wisest city official or employee refuses to express an opinion."

It was hardly unusual for stories about water to dominate the
city's newspaper columns. The amount of coverage reflected the
public's interest. In New York and Chicago, readers monitored
their stock prices. In San Diego they scoured the papers for the
regular runoff figures issued by the water department. It was

common knowledge that the city consumed roughly 6 million gallons of water a day.

The report went on to list Tuesday's readings from the city dams. The figures for Morena were the first since December 27. They confirmed what Seth Swenson had seen: the rain of New Year's Eve had been significant in the mountains. The creeks were flowing heavily. Just over 48 million gallons of water had flowed into the reservoir in eight days. The total was now up to 5.2 billion gallons.

The figures from elsewhere were also encouraging. The Upper and Lower Otay dams and the Sweetwater had registered healthy increases. Lower Otay had caught an extra 31 million gallons since December 27. The Dulzura conduit, linking Morena, Barrett, and the Otay dams, was also carrying water at a tremendous rate. It was delivering about 5.9 million gallons a day to the city—a day's supply, give or take a bath or two.

Theories about the method the mysterious rainmaker was employing were a dime a dozen. Stories of Dyrenforth-style explosions continued to fly around, despite Fred Binney's denials. He would quote Charles's reply to such claims: "Bombs, dynamite or other explosions, hydrogen balloons or any force of this kind I do not employ. I do not fight nature. I woo her through natural means."

With Charles's formula as great a secret now as in 1902, however, people still speculated on what these "natural means" were. Over the years, experts had likened Hatfield's method to a "sort of meteorological mustard plaster," a "chemical highly irritating to the elements." Others, familiar with rainmaking's past, made more educated guesses. John Bacon, the assistant public works manager, concluded that Hatfield's mixture was nothing more than "zinc on acid."

However, neither Bacon nor anyone else could deny that the rains had gotten Hatfield off to a good start. The *Union* took a pragmatic view of the situation that morning: "Whether

Hatfield's mysterious process is responsible for the downpour, he will get credit for it when next December the increase of water in Morena reservoir during the year is calculated."

FORECAST

San Diego, Thursday, January 6, 1916

Weather forecast for 12 hours ending 5 P.M. Thursday:
Unsettled weather.

—E. Herbert Nimmo, local forecaster,
United States Weather Bureau

THE WONDERFUL WEATHER FACTORY

[San Diego, Sunday, January 9, 1916]

D ean Blake cycled to work at his office in the Federal Building, on State and F streets, relishing the extra waves of greeting he seemed to be receiving from his fellow citizens. A studious-looking portrait of him, poised over a set of instruments, stared out from the front page of that morning's *San Diego Union*. The caption beneath read: ASSISTANT FORECASTER DEAN BLAKE READING THE TRIPLEOGRAPH.

The picture sat alongside other portraits, one of his boss, E. Herbert Nimmo, and another of his colleague, Earl Gildea, both engaged in what the paper called "typical scenes" at the weather bureau's offices on the third floor of the Federal Building. WONDERFUL "WEATHER FACTORY" INSTRUMENTS RECORD DATA, read one of the main headlines.

It had been Blake's father, Walter "Baldy" Blake, a former editor of the *Union*, who suggested he take the exam to join the United States Weather Bureau. Dean had struggled with grades at high school and was shocked to receive the highest marks of that year's applicants. He joined as a messenger boy in 1902 and spent the next thirteen years studying and working his way up to the role of assistant forecaster. His duties now ranged from maintaining the bureau's rooftop instruments to distributing its daily weather forecasts around the city on his bicycle.

Like his boss, Herbert Nimmo, Blake was sensitive to the bureau's reputation with the public. The impetus for its creation had been the devastating storms that hit the Great Lakes in 1868 and 1869. Both had arrived without warning, and 3,000 vessels and 530 lives were lost. Congress approved a national weather warning service the following year. At first it was little more than a series of observation stations linked by telegraph, producing brief forecasts and placed under the aegis of the U.S. Army Signal Corps. And for the bureau's first thirty years, any successes were offset by scandals and setbacks, particularly in the area of forecasting.

It didn't help that it had a tendency to shoot itself in the foot. One bureau chief in the Midwest wrote his forecasts five days in advance. He would head off to the mountains fishing, leaving the local telegraph office to wire one a day back to headquarters in Washington. Far more seriously, the bureau often failed to predict bad weather. On Monday, March 12, 1888, the forecast for New York City predicted "colder, fresher to brisk westerly winds, fair weather." The next day the city was hit by the worst blizzard in its history. Twenty-one inches of snow fell and two hundred people died. Most catastrophic of all, in September 1900, Isaac Cline, the bureau chief in the Texan port of Galveston, failed to spot the arrival of the worst hurricane in recorded history. Cline simply issued a conventional warning and the city got on with its Saturday. By Sunday morning, seven thousand people— including Cora, Cline's own pregnant wife—were dead.

It was little surprise that Charles Hatfield's generation put the bureau's meteorologists on a par with farmers who thought they could detect rain by the pain of the arthritis in their knees and placed their faith in time-honored sayings like "Clear moon, frost soon," "Red sky in the morning, sailor's warning, red sky at night, shepherd's delight," and "When birds and badgers are fat in October, expect a cold winter."

"Weather Guessers," they were routinely called. And guesswork was of little use to the nation.

Blake and Nimmo would often field angry phone complaints. "If it rained," Blake once observed, "but was not forecast and there was some inconvenience for people, or probably some of their plans were affected, they would vent their spite on the weather bureau. They'd sit down and write very nasty letters." The bile-filled missives were stuffed into a folder labeled "Crank File." "This was pretty full," he admitted.

So Blake was pleased at the article's attempt to "let down the veil which obscures the mysterious Mr. Nimmo, his assistants and his remarkable 'weather factory' from the public eye." The nerve center of the operation was what the paper called "the great tripleograph," a collection of meters and dials that, to the untrained observer's eye, at least, would not have looked out of place on the deck of Captain Nemo's *Nautilus*. The tripleograph was wired directly to the collection of anemometers, hygrometers, thermometers, and weather vanes on the roof of the Federal Building. In tones of quiet wonder, the article explained how Blake, Nimmo, and Gildea could sit at their desks and, "simply by pressing a button," watch a continuous flow of information about the direction and velocity of San Diego's winds, the exterior temperature, the duration of its sunshine, and—"when there is any"—the amount of rainfall.

Blake and Nimmo were particularly proud of their method for measuring rain, "a remarkable invention" called a "tipping bucket gauge." The twelve-inch gauge consisted of a receiving funnel mounted on an axis with a "tipping" mechanism. The axis balance was set up so that it rotated whenever the funnel contained .01 inch of rain. Each time it did so, an electrical connection would be made and the latest deposit recorded on the tripleograph downstairs. A spring would then send the funnel back to its upright position, ready for more rain. It was not the most overused of the bureau's instruments.

In the *Union* interview, Nimmo did his best to dispel any idea that his station was infallible. He and Blake were all too aware of the gaping holes in the bureau's forecasting armor and used the opportunity to warn of its limitations.

The bureau's Achilles' heel was storms from the southwest and the Pacific, he said. There were plans for a station in Ensenada, Mexico, but in the meantime he had to work with nothing but his barometer and the laws of logic.

"If no storms are reported by the northern bureaus and the barometer indicates stormy weather, it is taken as the logical solution that the storm is approaching from the south or southwest," he told the *Union*.

But, until more southerly stations were in place, San Diego was always going to be susceptible to unwelcome surprises from Mexico and the Pacific. "Frequently there is little indication of storms approaching from these directions," Nimmo lamented.

Nimmo knew the city's boosters saw San Diego's climate as its most powerful selling point. He did nothing to dent their civic sales drive, providing a raft of statistics that claimed, among other things, that the normal annual temperature was 61°F, that, on average, San Diego experienced just nine days a year without sunshine, and that thunderstorms were almost unheard of, occurring, on average, less than twice a year. The bureau's "tipping bucket" collected an average of just 10.91 inches a year, 90 percent of which fell between November 1 and May 1. San Diego's greatest monthly rainfall was 9.05 inches in February 1884. "Excessive rainfall, defined as more than 2.5 inches in 24 hours, has occurred but three times," he added.

The most glowing encomium came not from Nimmo but

from an American national hero, General Adolphus Greely, famous for surviving the ill-fated expedition to Lady Franklin Bay in the Arctic in 1881 and head of the Signal Corps, the forerunner of the U.S. Weather Bureau. "The American public is familiar on all sides with the elaborate and detailed statements of the weather at a thousand and one resorts. If we may believe all we read in such reports, the temperature never reaches the eighties, the sky is flecked with just enough of cloud to perfect the landscape, the breezes are always balmy and the nights are ever cool," he said in a statement to support Nimmo. "There is possibly one place in the United States where such conditions obtain—a bit of country about forty miles square at the extreme south western part of the United States in which San Diego County is located."

Greely's words underlined the universal feeling in the city. The main headline of the piece said it all: SAN DIEGO CLIMATE BEST IN WHOLE WORLD.

Dean Blake could have been forgiven for smiling ironically to himself that afternoon. Having placed such store in San Diego's lack of rain, the tripleograph readings and the bureau reports from San Francisco now pointed strongly toward a downpour. The low barometric pressure was consistent with the weather patterns to the north in Los Angeles and San Francisco. The bureau's strict forecasting rules allowed no room for elaboration. Bulletins conformed to short, often single-word headlines, but on this occasion, that seemed all that was required. As usual, it was Nimmo's name that was attached to the official bulletin for the twelve hours ending at 5:00 P.M. the next day. After closing down the office, Dean Blake pedaled his bicycle toward the waterfront wharves a few short blocks away and began circulating copies of the Weather Guessers' hunch: "Monday probably rain."

PART III

The Fulfillment [January 10–26, 1916]

"Rain, more rain." The streetlights reflect off the rain-soaked streets of
Broadway, San Diego, 1916. (San Diego Historical Society)

DELUGE

[Morena/San Diego, Monday, January 10, 1916]

W hen the clouds burst suddenly that morning, it was as if a faucet had been turned on in the sky.

Out on the lake at Morena, the rains came with such force that they churned the water's surface. On the northern ridge, sheltered under a canopy of cottonwood, Charles heard the first whisper of rain quicken and harden into an insistent susurrus. It must have sounded like the swelling of a distant applause.

Rather than relaxing, Charles rolled up his sleeves. He believed that even bursting clouds could be encouraged to deliver extra precipitation. One time he had arrived for a job during a healthy rainstorm and was confronted by a skeptical local official who wondered how he had the nerve to set up his tower when

Mother Nature was doing his work for him. "You may get three inches from this storm," Charles said, before heading off to find a suitable spot for his towers. "I could give you three and a half." He took the same view again.

The rain continued all afternoon. By the time he turned in for his usual nap, the rains were tumultuous. Beneath the canvas the sedulous drumbeat could only have eased Charles's descent into sleep.

It was his seemingly unquenchable optimism that had first won James Coffroth his nickname. A week into the New Year, however, "Sunny Jim"—like the ashen skies around him—was finding it hard to shine.

The son of one of California's first legislators, Coffroth had spent his life hovering on the edge of the law, initially as a boxing promoter. He had conned his way into his first match by posing as a telegraph messenger and went on to stage the famous 1903 rematch between "Gentleman Jim" Corbett and Jim Jeffries. In 1915, however, the California legislature had banned boxing. With what had looked like the sort of nifty footwork Jim Corbett could have used, Coffroth switched to horse racing and began building a track, the Lower California Jockey Club, near the tiny hamlet of Tijuana, a few hundred yards across the Mexican border.

Coffroth, a burly, back-slapping giant with a toothy Teddy Roosevelt grin, had chosen his location cannily. Racing and its evil twin, gambling, were being squeezed out of existence across America. Even in California, one of its last bastions, the storm clouds were gathering.

Tijuana was nothing more than a line of ramshackle adobe dwellings and a small trading post. Coffroth used the plentiful supply of cheap labor to carve out a mile-long oval track, enclosures, offices, and stables. As if to mock the lawmakers across the border, he built his rickety wooden grandstand so that it looked out over America, just four hundred yards away.

The buildings looked temporary but Coffroth was adamant

that he was in Tijuana to stay. His venture couldn't have gotten off to a better start. On New Year's Day, ten thousand people piled onto the San Diego & Arizona rail line for the short trip to the border. For many it was their first taste of Mexico. One visitor thought Tijuana looked like a "sleepy New England village."

Beneath blue gray skies and the fluttering green-and-white flags of the Mexican republic, Coffroth invited the governor of Lower California, Esteban Cantu, to declare racing open. The rains of New Year's Eve left the going heavy. As the horses slipped and sloshed their way around the first bend, Coffroth told Governor Cantu and his guests, "Races of these sort are the most entertaining. Why, one day in Nice, France, I saw the ponies plow through a regular lake of mud and water, which reached nearly to their knees, but it was rare good sport." The excitement of the day made the racing conditions matter less.

But the overcast weather and intermittent rain made the conditions more treacherous by the day. By Monday it was worse than ever.

The rains in the mountains poured through the creeks and gullies of the Cottonwood basin, north into Dulzura Creek and south into the Tecate and Tijuana rivers. From the foot of the mountains to the sea, the torrents of water dissolved the soil as if it were made of molasses and carved its way into gullies that hadn't seen water in a decade. The level of the Tijuana rose three feet that morning. The river was within a few hundred yards of the track's perimeter.

The rain reduced the number of visitors to a trickle. The racing they saw Monday afternoon degenerated into chaotic charges that owed more to the boxing rings than the so-called Sport of Kings. The smart money was being laid on whatever horse came out of starting gate number I. The gate gave jockeys a clear run on the driest part of the track. Gerald Baldwin, an oil deliveryman from San Diego, was visiting the track for the first time and couldn't believe what he was seeing. "They had six races and every horse that won was a Number One horse," he said. "He got out first and threw mud in their faces."

By now "Sunny Jim's" stock of excuses had run dry. He looked up at the leaden skies and prayed for the rain to end.

By early evening on the roof of the Federal Building the weather bureau's "tipping bucket" had adopted the manic rhythms of an overworked metronome.

The first 0.01 inch had registered on the tripleograph downstairs in the morning. As in the mountains, the rain had hardened into a rhythm that would not relent for hours.

Blake and Nimmo now learned that heavy rains were widespread along the Pacific Coast. The knowledge that the front was moving down from the northeast made their work more straightforward.

Both men were still basking in the extra attention the *Union* article had brought them. The normally taciturn Herbert Nimmo was so enamored by his sudden celebrity that he permitted himself a joke with the paper when it rang for his nightly weather report.

"Clear weather is indicated for tomorrow," he said. "We need the rain, but I guess a clear day now and then will be welcome. Patrons of the Tijuana racetrack will be glad of the change anyway."

MOVEMENT

[Dulzura, Tuesday, January 11, 1916]

I n the mountains, the sense of relief delivered by the break in the weather was short-lived.

Dorothy Clark Schmid knew the rainfall of the previous day was heavy but was still taken aback by the reading of the family rain gauge that morning. Her family had lived in the hills around Dulzura for thirty years. It was a tight-knit community of farmers and beekeepers, general-store owners and horsemen. Many, like Dorothy's father, were jacks-of-all-trades. An hour's drive from the city, the residents of Dulzura enjoyed the pioneering life, days that "began with hotcakes and ended with cribbage." Slowly, however, the road, rail, and water links to San Diego were drawing them into the city. Schmid's duties for the city included supervision of the road and recording rainfall.

Between December 15 and January 1, the family's gauge had collected 2.3 inches. On January 11, their gauge showed an accumulation of 0.86 inch of rain and runoff in the last 24 hours, in ordinary times a month's worth of rain.

Dorothy left home and saw the effect the rains were having. Dulzura Creek, sedate and shallow for long stretches at the end of December, had swollen into a fast-flowing stream. As the runoff of the previous day slid down the mountain, rocky stretches of the riverbed were turning into white-water torrents.

The rains were making the greatest impact on the steep, dusty gorges. Schmid saw that small landslides had begun. Gravity sent large deposits of loosened earth, overgrowth, and small boulders spilling into the valley bottom. "Hills could absorb no more and the earth, with its weight of brush and boulders, began to slip into the canyons below," she wrote in her diary.

For the rest of that day, Schmid, like everyone else in Dulzura, found herself watching the skies like a hawk.

CHECKERS
[Morena, Wednesday, January 12, 1916]

San Diego woke to a second consecutive day of clear cobalt skies—and newspapers dominated, once more, by water stories.

The first reported the latest developments in the city's ongoing legal battle with the water baron Colonel Ed Fletcher. Fletcher owned the Cuyamaca Water Company and the Flume Company and was trying to sell the city his "Volcan" water system, which involved the Cuyamaca Dam east of the city. The city—or more precisely, Fletcher's archrival, John Spreckels— wasn't interested and disputed Fletcher's rights to the part of his empire situated on the El Capitan Grande Indian reservation. The matter eventually landed in a Los Angeles courtroom. Naturally, the only real winner in the case was a lawyer. The case was polishing the reputation of San Diego's attorney, Terence Cosgrove, as the most formidable legal mind in the city.

It was the news from Morena and the backcountry reservoirs that really caught the eye. On Tuesday morning a brief report had mentioned the prodigious amounts of rain that fell at Morena between Saturday morning and Monday afternoon. More than 0.7 inch fell and 31.2 million gallons of runoff flowed into the reservoir. Today more detailed figures were released. They made for spectacularly good news. "According to figures compiled by statistician James Muirhead of the operating department the runoff at Morena has been 186,600,000 gallons of water this season as compared with only 84,500,000 gallons for the same period a year ago. . . . The rainfall on the Morena watershed so far this season is 20 per cent greater than for the corresponding period last season, but the runoff this year has been more than 125 per cent greater than in the winter of 1914–15."

The detailed figures were also intriguing. A large proportion of the season's rainfall had come in the last four days. In the fifty-six hours between Saturday morning and Monday afternoon, 31.2 million gallons had poured into Morena, a rate of more than 0.5 million gallons an hour. But between 7:00 A.M. Monday and 3:00 P.M. Tuesday, when it had stopped raining, the rate had trebled to 1.4 million gallons an hour. Morena was known for the slow rate at which runoff seeped down through the boulders, brush, and trees on its slopes. Muirhead ascribed the higher levels to the fact that Pine Creek and the Cottonwood had been flowing all winter and that the rains had been "bunched." Almost 45 million gallons—a quarter of that winter's total supply—had run into Morena in the last thirty-two hours.

As Herbert Nimmo predicted, the rain of Monday had passed, but there was still the whiff of more wet weather in the air. In the barbershops and saloons, many of San Diego's real weather experts were already wondering if the cause was something other than "bunching."

• • •

At his makeshift desk inside the A tent, Charles used the break in the weather to scribble letters to be taken back to the city by water department workers. He stayed in regular communication with Fred Binney, Mable, and his mother.

The tone of his missives was decidedly more upbeat than when he'd first arrived. Seth Swenson passed on news of another healthy rise in the runoff gauge that morning. Hatfield had more than made up for any lost ground at the beginning. He was in for the long haul, and just a few weeks ago he'd warned his family he might need to stay in the mountains all year. Now he began to express a quiet optimism that he'd see them much sooner than Christmas.

Paul understood how heavily the calendar was stacked against them. "We'd already lost November and December," he recalled later. Paul also understood how the pressure weighed on his brother's shoulders, and how it reflected in his temperament. So he knew when to stay out of the way, when to act as confidant. He also knew when to be a kid brother.

To ease the tension they'd play horseshoes, just as they had with their other brother Stephen at the apricot grove in Los Angeles. "It was good exercise," Paul said. Their other main source of entertainment was checkers, "lots of checkers." The outcome of their contests often hinged on how distracted Charles was. Paul could get himself into a winning position before his brother really concentrated. The more relaxed Charles was, the less Paul won. In the past few days, the younger Hatfield had barely won a game.

MUDDY BUSINESS

[San Diego, Thursday, January 13, 1916]

Around 11:00 A.M. the last vestige of blue sky disappeared behind the canopy of stratus cloud that had been sliding overhead all morning. It was soon dispensing overwhelming volumes of rain.

Reports of unusual rainfall began filtering into City Hall from across the county by noon. With each passing hour, the city's Public Works Department's files fattened with reports of leaking roofs, overwhelmed storm drains, and inundated cellars. Soaked wires and short-circuited junction boxes had slowed the electric trams to fits and starts. Phone lines faltered. Staring up from beneath storefront awnings downtown, people noticed that the clouds bore traces of livid purple. It was as if the very sky were bruised.

The heavy downpours of Monday had left the earth a dark, saturated brown. With the new rains, the soil quickly became saturated again. Citizens retreated into their homes rather than take to the waterlogged streets. "It was a clammy, messy, muddy business just to venture outdoors," said city attorney Shelley Higgins, who had no choice but to venture out. His route to City Hall, along G Street, now resembled a rice paddy.

By afternoon, hardware stores were doing a brisk trade in buckets, tubs, and any other containers capable of holding the rain. Marston's Department Store found plenty of buyers drawn by its latest advertisement for "New Cravenette Raincoats made of soft porous waterproof goods in tan and gray at $15, $18 or $20" and "Rubberized Raincoats in tan and gray, $6 up."

Others looked at the skies and despaired.

At the Isis Theater, the actor Walker Whiteside and his Metropolitan Company were already struggling to sell tickets for the first night of their tour on Friday. All over the city, posters modestly billed Whiteside's drama as "the most sensationally successful play the stage has known in twenty years." This may well have been true. But as the rains set in, Whiteside and his troupe quickly came to realize just how few people were going to brave the elements to watch a play called *The Typhoon*.

Wrapped in a raincoat and galoshes, Maggie Swenson picked her way toward the rainmaking tower. The rain was still pummeling the landscape, liquefying the soil and blackening the roots of the trees. At 7:00 A.M. that morning the Swenson gauge had edged its way to 199.19 feet. The reservoir had taken in a healthy runoff of 4 million gallons in the past twenty-four hours. Morena now held 5.29 billion gallons.

Maggie found Charles hard at work. He was sopping wet, rivulets of water running over the rim of his fedora and onto his face. His hair was plastered to his forehead and stuck out beneath the hat.

Maggie had received a phone call from someone she supposed

to be Charles's lawyer. It was probably Fred Binney. The message was to call him.

As usual, the exchange between Charles and Maggie was brief and awkward.

"It's sure raining now," she said to him.

"You haven't seen anything yet," Charles replied, his smile as unsettling and undecipherable as ever.

The roots of his confidence weren't really so obscure. His past successes owed much to his ability to read the long-term weather. Poring over the reports from the city at his makeshift desk in the A tent, the next few days' weather wasn't hard to predict.

Large swaths of America were experiencing an unusually cold winter. The *Union* carried weather bureau reports from Washington of extreme, often record-breaking cold in every state except Florida. Along the northwest coast, snows in Oregon and Washington State cut off train service and brought memories of the "big freeze-ups" of the 1870s and 1880s. In California, Sacramento was experiencing the "worst storm that has howled across the Sierras in the past half century." The bureau predicted that extreme cold would continue over almost all of the country for five days or longer. Their guidance influenced the weather forecast Herbert Nimmo had issued on Tuesday: "Fair, killing frost in exposed places Wednesday morning."

However, neither the city nor the county had seen frost. Only rain. As Charles looked out over the mountains, every bone in his body told him there was much more of it to come.

IS HATFIELD DOING IT?

[San Diego, Friday, January 14, 1916]

At the end of a day like the one she had just endured, Rose
Dysart would have given anything to relax and watch the last
sliver of sun setting over the Coronado peninsula. Instead, as
she looked out over the Pacific on the afternoon of Friday, January 14, 1916, all she could see was a gray so dull it might have
been made from the low-grade metal of a milking pail. It did
nothing to lift the mood inside her house. "It has rained all day
from six o'clock this morning," she scribbled in her diary.

At her home, a short walk from the Hotel del Coronado, Rose
had been up since 1:00 A.M. the previous night. She had spent the
small hours listening to her mother Adalaide's coughing spasms,
mopping her brow, adjusting her sleeping position, and feeding
her linctus or an extra spoonful of sleeping draught when the

113

attacks were severe. Perhaps it was the unremitting rain, but for some reason, Rose couldn't settle her down. "Mother was restless all night, cannot get her fixed so she is comfortable," she wrote. Things continued in this vein all day.

Rose had moved to San Diego with her mother and Rose's sister, Martha, from St. Louis after the death of her father, Andrew Dysart, in January 1903. Doctors said San Diego's climate might ease Adalaide's bronchial problems, and Martha's husband, George Allen, recommended the move. Allen died soon after their arrival, however, leaving the women to fend for themselves.

As the youngest child, and a spinster to boot, Rose inevitably took on the heaviest of the duties. Martha and her niece Helen shared the chores as much as they could. But Martha suffered from neuralgia and now even Helen had come down with a cold, brought on by the dampness outside. Rose often joked that the house had become "a regular hospital." It would seem even more so when the special hospital bed she had ordered her mother arrived later that week.

The family doctor came by at 2:00 that afternoon only to find Rose's mother sleeping. Adalaide later claimed she was awake and had overheard the doctor asking "what's that funny noise she's making?" He promised to come back later but with the light fading it was clear the weather had beaten him. In summer, the Pacific winds could waft the sounds of the surf on the Coronado strand through the Dysarts' open windows. Today, however, the northwesterlies merely rattled and whistled through the shutters, a noisy accompaniment to the drumming of the rain on the glass outside.

By the time supper was finished, Adalaide was already asking for her bed. After the restlessness of the previous night, she wanted to sleep propped up by cushions in the morris chair in the living room. Rose sat with her, talking quietly to Helen in the evening gloom.

Already Rose's thoughts were beginning to echo those of many San Diegans. Her grasp of the details was sketchy, but from the few conversations she'd had with friends and neighbors, she knew what—or more precisely, who—people were blaming for the intensity and stubbornness of the rain: "A man—Hatfield—told the city he would fill the Morena dam for $10,000 and to get rid of him they told him to go ahead so he built him a shack up there and is using chemicals to make it rain," she wrote in her diary. "I suppose he really thinks he is doing it."

Inside City Hall, a small group of councilmen stared out at the rain lashing across G Street. They were finally acknowledging the question half the city was asking.

"Is Hatfield doing it? I don't think so, but I hope he is," Councilman Fox responded when asked his view by a reporter from the *Union*.

By early evening, the rhythm of the rain had, if anything, hardened. Outside on G Street, cars and trams plowed through the ankle-deep waters, leaving a sludge-brown slop on the sidewalks behind them. On the city's unpaved roads and alleyways, tires spun and sprayed mud in all directions. Few people were out on foot.

The gathering of councilmen included most of the five who had voted to put Charles to work. Warming to the conversation with the *Union* reporter, they mixed caution with a touch of levity.

"It is fine rain, any way you put it," remarked Otto Schmidt, one of the four who had voted for hiring the rainmaker.

"Here's hoping that it continues to rain so hard that Hatfield will have to build an ark," observed another, Percy Benbough.

Herbert Fay, the sole dissenter in December, merely nodded and added a solemn "Amen."

The councilmen had treated the Hatfield motion much the same way ever since Charles set off for Morena. During a debate on Colonel Fletcher's offer to sell water from the San Diego River to the city, Percy Benbough got a big laugh by suggesting the water baron "refer it to Hatfield."

Now they weren't so sure it was a laughing matter. "You will remember that some of us were once inclined to laugh at wireless telegraphy and other really great inventions," said Fox. "Far be it from me to laugh at Hatfield. Let him go to it. If he makes good, all the better."

The tangible tide of sympathy now flowing toward Charles didn't go down well at the Federal Building. There was a snippiness in Herbert Nimmo's voice when the *Union* turned up to ask his view of the rain that evening. He again refused to grant the rainmaker the oxygen of publicity. "Mr. Nimmo said he would reserve his official opinion until some future date," the *Union* man recorded.

At least Nimmo was willing to volunteer one opinion. "I'll tell you what I think," he bridled, "I think that we are going to have more rain tomorrow and that the man who leaves his umbrella at home when he comes to work Saturday morning will be making a mistake."

"FORKED TONGUE"

[City Hall, Saturday, January 15, 1916]

erence Cosgrove arrived at his City Hall office carrying a
rain-sodden umbrella, a dampened copy of the *Union*, and a
growing realization that as San Diego's city attorney, he had
to address the thorny issue of Rainmaker Hatfield.

People's opinion of Cosgrove generally turned on whether he
was for or against them in court. To those on his side, the unflap-
pable, eloquent Notre Dame University and Yale Law School
graduate was not just one of the sharpest legal minds in the state
but a thorough gentleman. "A wonderful man," his longtime secretary, Mable Slocum, called him.

To opponents, however, Cosgrove seemed one step removed
from an alley cat. By December 1915, his battle of wills with Ed
Fletcher over the El Capitan water rights had become intensely

personal. When Cosgrove's name came up in conversation the water baron tended to reach for the language of a dime novel. To Fletcher, the attorney "talked with a forked tongue."

Cosgrove's chosen specialty had done nothing to hinder his rise through the California legal ranks. He was an acknowledged expert in water rights, with a growing reputation for solving intractable problems. In 1914 he wrote a brilliant opinion claiming San Diego had the right to access the San Diego River. His argument drew on Spanish and Mexican law, which he said should hold in the modern United States. (It would become the basis of a landmark victory a decade later.) He was using the same principle in his case against Fletcher.

With such lofty matters on his mind, it was perhaps not surprising that the thirty-four-year-old advocate had given Charles Hatfield barely a second's thought. His only contribution to the December meeting was a response to a question about the legality of any contract with Hatfield. His reply had been a model of legal obliqueness.

"If Hatfield fills Morena, I guess there would be no doubts about the legality," he said. The *Union* reporter present recorded the important detail that Cosgrove delivered his verdict with a "Sphinx-like grin."

The fact that no formal contract had actually been signed had pushed the matter even further to the back of his mind.

The unrelenting rhythm of rain on his office window now dragged it back to the front.

Far from abating, the rain had intensified through the night. In the dreary light of morning, Cosgrove sidestepped his way through a landscape of submerged sidewalks, overflowing storm drains, and muddied pools of standing water.

Over breakfast he read the latest rain and water figures. Both confirmed the intensity of the rain on Friday. More than 0.5 inches of rain had fallen in the city itself. Once more, however, the greatest impact was felt in the backcountry. At the Lower Otay Dam, 0.41 inches of rain produced an extra 10 million gallons of runoff. Supplies there now looked so healthy that the water department released 2 million gallons for consumption by the city. Morena's figures stood out even more. In the eight hours between 7:00 A.M. and 3:00 P.M., 1.2 inches of rain fell and 26.39 million gallons of new runoff accumulated. Water had been pouring in at a rate of well over 3 million gallons an hour.

The newspapers were now openly linking the tumult with the tower at Morena. IS RAINMAKER AT WORK? RAIN EXCEEDS NORMAL ran the *Union* headline above a report that also gave an account of the previous day's conversations in the corridors outside Cosgrove's office. For a civil servant, Terence Cosgrove possessed acutely tuned political antennae. Everything he saw told him he needed to act.

Cosgrove quickly assessed the strengths and weaknesses of the city's case. Clearly the biggest positive was that there was no signed contract. Also, Charles had confused the issue by making three separate offers. The council hadn't accepted any of them formally.

Yet there was no doubt that Hatfield had been given some sort of "implied contract." At the meeting it was clear that the motion passed by the majority was for the third and simplest option: filling Morena for $10,000. This was widely reported in the city press, as was the specific target of 10 billion gallons of water. A good lawyer might be able to make it stick.

To Cosgrove, however, the city's greatest advantage lay in the sheer unprovability of any case Hatfield might bring. Cosgrove knew every judge in California. None of them was the kind of man to rule that a rainmaker and not the Almighty had been responsible for bringing on these rains.

Nevertheless, the situation required action. That morning Cosgrove dashed off a letter to Hatfield, care of Fred Binney. The attorney instinctively knew that the more detail was revealed, the more leeway he would have to question the rainmaker's method and its effectiveness. The letter amounted to a fishing expedition. Cosgrove asked Charles for details "concerning plans, number of men employed, methods used." Later that day, collared by the small posse of reporters lurking in the corridors of City Hall, Cosgrove stuck to the line he had fixed on that morning: "He will not be required to reveal any secrets, but he must furnish such information as will enable the city to ascertain whether or not the runoff at Morena is the direct result of the rainmaking efforts." This time no one detected the Sphinx-like smile.

Up in Balboa Park, the Exposition's garrison of Marines, Cavalry, and Coast Guard Artillery was being reinforced by a small army of painters, carpenters, bricklayers, and background artists. None of them could fix the cracks starting to appear in the great fair's self-confidence.

Announcements about the various countries to be represented at the new "international" version of the fair had been coming thick and fast since New Year's Eve, when Aubrey Davidson, the event's president, had announced the biggest coup of all. With the telegram from Paris's ambassador to the United States in his hand, Davidson confirmed that France was lending the city its famous Luxembourg art collection. The eighty or so paintings by Monet, Bonnard, and Degas were worth half a million dollars and would fill two halls. Similar offers soon poured in from Spain, the Netherlands, Japan, Persia, Egypt, Siam, Java, Luxembourg, Australia, and South Wales.

Before the rain started, Davidson had pledged that the new exhibits would open to the public on February 15. Teams of tradesmen were working around the clock, throwing up new walls, designing new displays and backdrops, and generally polishing up the place. The construction forced Davidson to close many buildings to the public. Now he worried that the turnstiles would completely grind to a halt.

Davidson's salesmen were under orders to give the fair's "Garden of Eden" the hardest sell. Inspired by London's Kew Gardens and located in San Diego's Balboa Park, the botanical garden consisted of 1,400 acres of newly planted trees, from acacias and eucalyptus to cedars and araucarias, and more than a million shrubs, from dracaenas and nolinas to strelitzias and agaves. The rose garden alone boasted 7,000 bushes. The Exposition was so proud of the park that its organizers launched a special monthly magazine, *California Garden*, to promote the vast array of horticultural events.

Yet an article in that morning's *Union*, written by an Exposition booster, illustrated the faint air of desperation the salesmen were beginning to adopt. "The grounds were never so beautiful as now since the rains have made the flora and foliage more luxuriant and more brilliant in coloring."

It didn't work. The turnstiles failed to click that morning.

BEYOND HEARSAY

[Dulzura, Sunday, January 16, 1916]

Dean Blake and Herbert Nimmo spent the morning distracted by the constant ringing of the weather bureau's two telephones. The calls were the usual blend of abuse and curiosity. Many callers mentioned Hatfield and echoed the sentiments of a letter the *Union* ran in Sunday's paper. It read simply: "For the love of Mike, call him off."

The weather was bringing San Diego's life to a standstill. All of the city's baseball diamonds were swamped, and three big games, one of which involved the crew of the newly docked USS *Oregon*, were abandoned. "It is unlikely that any athletic contests will be staged today," the *Union* reported solemnly.

The newest water figures confirmed that the storm was increasing in strength. The latest totals were for the thirty-two hours ending at 3:00 Saturday afternoon. In that time, the city's system had taken in an extra 153 million gallons of water.

There were eye-catching gains at the Lower Otay Dam. Weeks earlier, the reservoir had measured thirty feet across and was barely a few inches deep—more a puddle than a lake. At 3:00 P.M. that afternoon the dam's supervisor, Rudolph Wueste, phoned with news that the level had risen by 5 inches in eight hours. Now it was a lake. The figures for Morena provided the really spectacular reading. At 7:00 A.M. Sunday morning, Seth Swenson's rain gauge topped 124 inches. The dam now held more than 6.3 billion gallons. During the last thirty-two hours, the mountain dam's rain accounted for more than three-quarters of the city's total impoundment—just over 119 million gallons.

By late afternoon, Walter Bellon's hired Model T was bucking and sliding all over the crumbling backcountry roads. Bellon worked at the health department and had heard all manner of rumors over the past forty-eight hours. He was fed up with the tall stories and had hired the car so he could establish the facts for himself—"beyond hearsay." After traveling thirty miles of washed-out roads toward Morena, his path was obstructed.

The rains had by now loosened vast screes of earth and boulders. The molten mudslide was moving down the foothills. Like a sea of lava, it had covered large sections of the road. Bellon pressed on briefly, skirting his way along the patches of clear road. But with each fresh slide the conviction grew that he needed to head back.

"I retreated as fast as the rough road would permit," he said afterward. "As luck would have it, the road that I had just traveled a few minutes before was slowly being blocked. If I had waited a few minutes longer to turn back, this slow-moving mass of earth could easily have crushed and carried my rented auto into the deep canyon below."

On his way back, he met another driver in similar retreat. He had been trying to reach Morena via Buckman Springs. But that road was also washed out. The great dam was cut off.

At the Federal Building, Nimmo and Blake scanned the afternoon's reports from Washington and San Francisco and concluded that an end to the rain was now within sight.

In the late afternoon, Nimmo issued a forecast for the twelve hours to 5:00 P.M. Monday. "Unsettled weather, with occasional rain." As Dean Blake cycled home that evening, dropping off copies of the forecast as he went, he was almost a lone figure on the streets.

By nightfall, an eerie silence had settled over the city. The Western Union telegraph lines to Los Angeles went down shortly after midnight. Within a couple of hours, the city's three other services—the Postal Telegraph Company, the Pacific Telephone and Telegraph Company, and the Home Telephone Company—failed, too. At the offices of the *Union* on 2nd Street, the lines lasted long enough for a steady flow of callers to paint a picture of the disaster now unfolding.

At 2:00 A.M. farmer Harry Lewis telephoned with the news that the San Diego River had burst its banks. The heavily populated Mission Valley and Old Town areas were in danger from the fast-rising floodwaters. At around the same time, word arrived that the city engineer, Fred Lockwood, had roused a team of engineers and was fighting to save the link to the main road north, the concrete bridge at Old Town.

The bad news wasn't confined to the city and its immediate suburbs. From the north, in San Dieguito, ranchers called in to report that the river there had broken its banks. In the southeast, at San Ysidro, there were reports of the Tijuana River surging, too.

At 4 A.M., Walter Bellon was awakened by a call from the city's isolation hospital on the north side of the river. The waters were climbing fast, he was told. The patients would have to be evacuated.

As Bellon drove through the dark and deserted streets, the rising water reached the floorboards of his Model T. Crossing the river he saw truckloads of sandbags being unloaded by Fred Lockwood and his team. They were reinforcing the approaches to the concrete bridge.

At the hospital, Bellon found the water over seven feet deep on the ground floor. He helped move the hospital's eighteen patients to an old house on higher ground.

Across the bay, Lewis Weston sat bolt upright in his bed, trying to make sense of the hellish noises being carried on the wind. "During the night we heard a terrible roar," he recalled. "I mean it was fantastic." Weston and his family guessed the noise was coming from farms on the opposite side of the valley. Peering out through the gloom they saw enough to guess at what was unfolding. "We saw a light go out in one house. We figured, oh, there's been a landslide and they have been wiped out."

A STATE OF FLOOD

[San Diego, Monday, January 17, 1916]

L it by a still-invisible sun, the morning sky emerged as a rumpled
blanket of grays and charcoals. For the fifth day in succession,
the clouds were dispensing a dense sheet of rain that seemed to
be washing away all shape and color. The world had been reduced
to shades from the same dismal palette, and in the murky light,
earth and sky seemed indivisible. It was soon clear why.

The extent of the flooding took people's breath away. In Mission Valley, the water stretched bluff to bluff, almost a mile
across. The main railway line, the Santa Fe, was underwater.
Houses built on the valley floor were circled by a roiling mass of
water. Under the surface of the water, fields of submerged alfalfa
crops swayed like seaweed beds in the turbulence.

Lewis Weston rose at first light and discovered that the railway line had been engulfed. Freight cars full of sand were "brushed aside like they were toothpicks." Yet the house across the valley survived. There had been a landslide, but it split either side of the promontory, miraculously saving the home. Weston's gaze soon moved down into the valley where the stream had turned into a torrent, carrying huge waves. One was so high it obscured the other riverbank, another bore vast watering troughs, and another carried "a haystack with chickens and little animals on top, riding down the river."

Farther up the valley, Rose Schiller was counting the number of homes she had seen floating by her window. At one point she left her parlor, which had the best view over the valley. She asked her husband Leo to let her know what happened while she was gone. "When I came back three were gone. He'd looked the other way and missed seeing them."

All over the city, people fought the liquidized landscape. "The dirt was like quicksand. Even on the hillsides it was awful and heavy rocks would just let go and come rolling down the mountain," recalled Elihu Martin, whose farm near Descanso was in the path of the water that came down from Cuyamaca. Martin struggled to lead his cattle to safety. "The cattle would bog down on the hillsides and you couldn't get to them by horseback. We used to go in on foot and tie their legs together and roll them out of that boggy place and pull them down the hill. Sometimes they would get right up and take after you and then they would run back into the bog again and get bogged down."

Many farmers were denied a chance to rescue their animals. Small flotillas of bloated carcasses were already sailing down Mission Valley toward the ocean.

People took refuge wherever they could.

From the safety of the rafters of their barn in the Sorrento Valley, the Diffendorf family watched in awed silence. "We could see all kinds of things floating down," recalled Grace Diffendorf, "automobiles, timbers, chairs and tables, barns where they stored the apples taken from the orchards, chicken coops. The debris stuck in the tops of the willow trees."

"Riding Down the River." A house floats down a flooded Mission Valley, January, 1916. (San Diego Historical Society)

Not everyone was able to escape. From his home on higher ground in Escondido, Clarence Rand saw the water swallowing up a two-story brick house farther down the hill. Then he glimpsed "a woman and her three or four children that were in the upstairs window hollering for help." Rand drove his pair of old plow horses to their rescue. "The lower story was half-full of water. They came down the stairs and were wading in the water clear up to their waists. They came to the side window, got on my horses and we got out."

The scenes of chaos in the country were mirrored in the downtown district. Cars were abandoned in the mud. Canoes carved their way down Broadway, ferrying the stranded to dry ground. Some people walked the streets waist-deep in water, dodging pieces of lumber, felled telegraph poles, and the detritus of dissolving homes. Underneath the water, lighter objects swilled around before being carried along by the current. The air was mildewed, faintly rotten.

Many were lucky to escape alive. In the neighborhood of Riverside, it took three attempts to rescue a family of four, including a mother, cradling a baby in her arms, who had spent all day in a tree. The family was too petrified to climb into a flat-bottomed skiff. They were eventually winched to safety on a one-inch rope attached to the tree.

The occupants of the city dog pound were less fortunate. Superintendent Joe Mutters was downtown when he heard that the water was surging. He rushed back in his car to find his home and the pound being washed away. Mutters swam out to rescue the sixteen dogs in his care. Only one, a cocker spaniel, was alive. He swam back to safety with it under his arm. The rest perished.

Herbert Nimmo thought this was an example of the city's rains being condensed into one tumultuous burst. "It is unusual, although not altogether unprecedented that San Diego's rain should come all at the same time," he said that afternoon. His tripleograph registered readings beyond anything he'd ever seen. Winds from the south that day were timed at thirty-eight miles per hour. The volume of water passing through his tipping gauge was unprecedented. "The records, when compiled, should show that the storm just about sets a record for these parts."

He issued his weather forecast for Tuesday with a hint of resignation. The previous night's forecast now seemed wildly optimistic. This time he erred on the side of pessimism. Dean Blake distributed copies of the forecast as best he could. It read: "Rain tonight, and probably tomorrow."

Gerald Baldwin took his truck down to Tijuana with his usual delivery of stove oil and distillate. He saw the damage the rains were causing as he crossed a small bridge near the San Diego and Arizona railway line. A group of jockeys from the racetrack waved him down; they were heading for higher ground on the other side of what had been a small stream but was now a seething river.

"My truck had a running board on it and about a dozen jockeys got on the truck and rode down with me," he recalled. "I came across a little bridge just west of the culvert under the San Diego and Arizona tracks. One of the jockeys tapped me on the shoulder and said 'look back there.' And the bridge had gone out just after we had crossed it. If it had gone out ten or fifteen seconds before that we would all have gone down the creek."

Baldwin had visited the track on Sunday and was amazed to find racing still going on. "The water running down to the grandstand where they made the bets was ankle deep," he recalled.

This time he found racing abandoned. Hordes of workers were sandbagging the saddling enclosure and the stands. Teams of men with shovels were attempting to divert the water from the track itself, but with little success.

He made his delivery and headed back to the main bridge across the Tijuana as fast as he could. On the road he came across a well-dressed man in a Buick stranded in the mud.

> He was dickering with some Mexican to pull the car out of the river. First the Mexican offered to pull it out for $5. In about five minutes the water was up to the running board and the owner started to give him $5 and the Mexican said "No, $10." And he wouldn't pay that.
>
> The water got higher still, so then he came back and offered the Mexican $15 and the Mexican says "too late." That Buick was sunk right down in the sand and six months later somebody was over there and found the top of it.

Baldwin didn't hang around to watch. He throttled his truck through the mud and made it across the bridge over the Tijuana. "I was the last person that came over that bridge before it went out."

Late in the afternoon, Charles left Paul at the tower and made his way down to the Swensons' cottage.

His optimism had been growing all day. At 7:00 A.M. that

morning, Seth Swenson's rain gauge showed a level of 124.19 feet—an increase of more than 4 feet since Sunday morning. Around 910 million gallons had poured into the reservoir the previous day. That meant Morena now contained 6.385 billion gallons. However, it was the news from San Diego that got him really excited. It also made him uneasy.

Since his earliest run-ins with George Franklin in Los Angeles, Hatfield had been wary of people—and the weather bureau in particular—deflecting the credit away from him. He decided it was time for a statement, another "I did it."

He didn't want to get involved in talking to the newspapers. He guessed the news would seep out somehow, so he dialed the water impoundment department number Seth rang with his twice-daily reports.

A clerk picked up the phone to hear the mysterious man of the moment at the other end of the scratchy line.

"I just wanted to tell you that it is only sprinkling now," Charles announced.

It took the official a moment to form a reply.

"Are you kidding?" he asked eventually.

"Never more serious in my life," Charles said. "Just hold your horses until I show you a real rain."

Then the line went out.

Charles's PR anxieties would have been eased if he knew how the rain—and he—were now being received in the city.

The front-page headline of the *Union* that morning read: DOWNPOUR LAYS MANTLE OF WEALTH ON COUNTY: RAIN RECORDS SMASHED. But it was in the lengthy article that followed, seemingly based on a phone conversation with the Swensons, that the paper talked of Charles in the most serious terms yet:

> The mysterious Hatfield, rainmaker, was said to be par-
> ticularly active in the vicinity of Morena, Sunday. While
> engaged in his experiments, Hatfield is not altogether

sociable, but persons watching his work from a distance said he seemed to be on the job all hours of the day and considers the downpour due to his efforts. Incidentally, it was said that Hatfield himself is getting a good soaking.

Hatfield's name was on almost every tongue in San Diego yesterday. Many were inclined to jest when his operations were mentioned, but all agreed that things were coming his way. And there were many others, cooped up in their homes, or wading about the streets with umbrellas, who have begun to take the Morena dam's "rainmaker's" pact with the city seriously.

Charles's case was being taken so earnestly, in fact, that one of the city's senior judges, Justice Solon Bryan, felt compelled to weigh in on the rainmaker's side. A veteran of the Civil War, Bryan was a disciple of the old Edward Powers doctrine. "It is a fact that after practically every great battle of the Civil War, a thunder shower followed," the justice said in his office that morning. "Whether it was because of the amount of saltpeter or some other chemical used or because of the battle smoke, I do not know, I am sure. Hatfield probably does."

The judge sensed the weight of evidence leaning in Charles's favor. "It sounds reasonable to me that he has some kind of rain producing chemical up his sleeve. Anyway, it looks as if he will collect from the city, whether or not they are able to make him prove definitely that he is responsible for the rain."

For once it was Fred Binney who sounded the lone note of caution. Binney called Hatfield to express his concern about the lack of a contract. He suggested that Charles come back down to the city to sort the matter out with Terence Cosgrove now, before things went too far. Charles dismissed the idea. He would come down when the dam was full. Binney was unable to shake his uneasy feeling, but from then on he kept it to himself.

• • •

Charles's conversation with the water clerk was relayed to the *Union* and reported in that evening's edition. The report only added to the newspaper's frustration at not having a reporter on the spot at Morena. In the mayor's chamber, it nudged the political barometer to Stormy.

Sensing the public mood, council member Walter Moore announced he had seen enough to be satisfied of Charles's cause. Cosgrove should stop his attempts to extract details of the rainmaking operation via Fred Binney.

"I'm willing to credit him with this storm without forcing him to expose his rainmaking secrets," the mayor told the council chamber that morning. But Herbert Fay, the sole objector to the original vote on Hatfield, was still against it. He demanded to know whether the city should "pay out public moneys for the alleged or assumed accomplishments of any work or works that has for its object and as a basis for its accomplishments the utilizing of the natural laws of the universe."

The next move, everyone knew, would be Terence Cosgrove's. Privately, Cosgrove had left no one in any doubt about his feelings. The rain was an act of God—both in actuality and, more importantly, legally. In his conversation with council members, he adopted the patient, vaguely patronizing tone of a Harvard law professor explaining torts to an undergraduate. "He cannot collect for what would happen without his agency," he argued. "If you contract to pay a tailor $50 for a suit of clothes to be made and delivered to your home by another tailor, the first one cannot collect from you."

Cosgrove was already calculating the dangers implicit in accepting that the rainmaker was responsible for the rains at Morena and in the city. The council of San Diego County had already estimated the cost of broken roads and bridges and was hinting that it might sue the city for hiring Hatfield. However, the county sensed the legal difficulty. "If a suit were started against the city for damages due to the storm, anyone starting such a suit would have to prove that Hatfield and his contract with the city did have something to do with the rains," said District Attorney Marsh. "It might be difficult to get a judge and jury to believe this. And yet if the city pays Hatfield $10,000 this would possibly be a step in the direction of establishing proof."

Local businessman Charles Cristadoro had anticipated Cosgrove's thinking in a letter to the *Union*: "If the Morena dam 'goes out' can 'Rainmaker' Hatfield be held for damages?" he asked. "Before this thing goes on much longer had he better not enter into a good and sufficient bond?"

To head off any further difficulties, Cosgrove drafted a contract that covered every eventuality. Rather than talking in general terms of filling Morena, the contract specifically required Charles to place "an additional 10 billions of gallons of water" in the reservoir. It also included a clause asking Charles to "hold the City blameless from all actions for damages arising out of the performance of the work to be done under this contract, and to defend at his own cost any and all such actions, and to secure indemnity insurance."

Cosgrove knew there was no way on earth Hatfield would sign it.

As the councilmen dispersed that evening, rumors of Cosgrove's intentions flew across the city. They did not go over well.

The worst of the rains seemed to be over, and the city's dams were brimming with fresh water. Sympathy for Charles was running as high as the San Diego River. At the *San Diego Sun*, the paper's poet in residence was already at work on an ode to be published the following morning.

> The council from its seat on high,
> Made a contract with a guy
> To fill Morena to the brim,
> So no more water would stay in.
>
> Ten thousand bones was the amount,
> They agreed to pay him on account.

"Sure," said Hatfield, "I'll take the bet,
And three to one you'll all get wet."

Soon one morning they awoke,
To find it really was no joke.
The fellow's tip was safe and sane—
For just look out, and see it rain.

Rain Friday, Saturday, Sunday too;
Council starts to fret and stew;
Monday, rain to their great sorrow;
Forecast says, more rain tomorrow.

The city attorney was asked for advice,
"Oh," says he, "I'll fix that in a trice.
That contract, you know, was all a joke;
At any rate, the bank is broke."

Now come on fellows, you took the dare!
Show your hand up, fair and square.
If he has you beaten, take your pill:
The taxpayer must foot the bill.

Ahead of this, the *Sun's* evening's edition retold another tale of a city that reneged on its deal with a miracle worker.

The headline read: A STORY ABOUT THE PIED PIPER OF OLD, THE HATFIELD OF HIS DAY.

The paper rehashed Robert Browning's children's rhyme of the ratcatcher and the duplicitous burghers of Hamelin. "People waiting with interest to see what the city council will do if Rainmaker Chas M. Hatfield comes for his $10,000 recall Browning's famous story," the front-page piece began. The paper was worried at what might happen if Hatfield was cheated like the Pied Piper. "Now if the San Diego council doesn't give Hatfield that 10,000 guilders? Oh, pshaw, say it yourself."

ATLANTIS

[San Ysidro, Tuesday, January 18, 1916]

The lunchtime edition of the *San Diego Sun* confirmed the news that the storm had—indirectly—claimed its first death. George W. Rainsberger, an employee of the City Works Department, had spent all night working to save his own home and those of others in the Chollas Valley. Early in the morning, he collapsed. The coroner blamed his death on heart failure brought on by exposure.

The news—not to mention the irony of the poor victim's name—only added an even darker edge to the gallows humor now spreading through the populace. The *Sun*'s front-page summary began that morning:

San Diego was shut off completely from the outside world as Tuesday dawned. The Southland Exposition city might as well have been on an island in the mid-Pacific as far as communications with the rest of the U.S. was concerned. Not a train entered or left the city. Not a wire, telephone or telegraph was working. Peace terms might have been signed, bringing the European war to an end, and San Diego would not have heard of it.

One thousand eastern millionaires might have been in Los Angeles, waiting to come and buy our real estate and they couldn't have reached us. The letters from those back east, sweethearts had to wait—there was no mail. San Diegans were alone to the world with only their thoughts, their rain and a busy man named Hatfield.

Underpinning the mood was a feeling that the short-term damage was far outweighed by the long-term benefits the billions of gallons of impounded water would bring. "There were ten optimists to every pessimist on the streets of San Diego," reported the *Union*. "The great catchment is generally considered to have offset a hundredfold all the damage to property. The runoff into the reservoirs will also continue giving city and county a wealth of water for future use, and bringing with it the happiness and prosperity that is only possible through such bountiful water supply."

The water department wasn't arguing with that view "It means dollars to the city," said Fred Lockwood, the city's manager. "Let 'er rain."

The rain wasn't harming business in the city's hotels, either.

Over Christmas and New Year's the society columns of the *San Diego Union* had recorded the influx of guests arriving "to join the winter colony" at hotels like the St. James, the U.S. Grant, and the del Coronado.

Now the well-heeled guests at the U.S. Grant relaxed in the Turkish Hammam Baths and the Salt Water Plunges, played billiards and drank in the Bivouac Grill. Less refined hotels staged special concerts and afternoon tea dances. One astutely capitalized on the closure of the Tijuana track by installing a mechanical horse racing set and staging indoor racing in its lobby. "I'm betting on Hatfield," one guest was reported as saying.

"What's the dope?" asked another.

"Greatest long shot California's ever seen. Tore up the track at Tijuana, turned the bookies' ring upside down, and closed down racing for Coffroth till tomorrow."

"Never heard of the horse."

"Horse, he's no horse. Hatfield the rainmaker. I'm betting he'll win over the City Council."

The tone wouldn't last the day, especially down at the border.

The news started sweeping through the valley of the Tijuana River early that morning. The river—already swollen and dense with sand, scrub, and sections of trees—had risen dramatically and was now surging through the creeks, heading west to the ocean. In the village of San Ysidro, the commune its three hundred families liked to call the "True Arcadia" was being transformed into Atlantis.

The commune was founded eight years earlier, when William E. Smythe, a goateed newspaperman and historian had addressed a crowded Garrick Theatre in San Diego. A disciple of the progressive socialist Bolton Hall, Smythe appealed to those Americans desperate to leave "the rush, turmoil and uncertainty of the city" for a simpler, healthier existence working an acre of land. Smythe's argument was summed up in one of his favorite phrases: "A little land and a living, surely, is better than a desperate struggle and wealth—possibly."

Smythe's speech instantly hit a nerve. By the end of 1908, a small group of pioneers had paid between $200 and $350 for plots of land ranging from 150 feet by 40 feet to an acre within sight of the Mexican border. Each agreed to the same terms: planting grass and flowers, building their houses thirty feet from the front boundary, and promising not to "manufacture or sell intoxicants" on their property. Smythe and his supporters also promised that no "Mexicans, Mongolians or Negroes" would acquire lots.

Around San Diego, the community became known as the "Little Landers." By 1915 the land provided a living for more than three hundred families. Their produce was trucked twice daily to their own market in San Diego. "It was pure communism, the idealistic, not the Russian kind," said one resident.

The original community had settled on an elevated mesa above the river itself. With each passing year, however, as the levels of the Tijuana remained low, new arrivals edged down toward the river itself. The barren, scrub-infested flats were transformed into green fields and goat pastures, berry patches, and orchards of figs, oranges, lemons, guavas, apricots, and peaches.

At first light that morning, not a single square foot of the crop was visible beneath the roiling brown water.

The scramble out of the low-lying land had begun early. William Hevener had built a good life for himself rearing chickens. He and his wife grabbed every valuable they could. "I loaded a wheelbarrow," he said. "And headed to higher ground." From the slopes he watched helplessly as eight years of work was washed away in minutes.

James Russell Johnson's father had sold many of the families' homes. He watched bungalow after flimsy bungalow perform the same pathetic dance of defiance. "Those old houses would just start to wobble a little bit and pretty soon they'd just roll over and down the river they went," said Russell, who watched the carnage from the safety of his goat dairy. "It just scooped up all of those places."

News of the Little Landers' plight soon reached San Diego. At noon, the city's sheriff and a party of U.S. Navy volunteers arrived in a flotilla of boats. They spent the afternoon hauling families off rooftops and plucking people from the upper branches of the few trees that had been strong enough to withstand the water.

• • •

The floodwaters had seeped over the San Diego and Arizona railway line that ran to the border and Tijuana. One of the last trains to make it down had delivered ten thousand bags of sand to Jim Coffroth.

By midmorning, the bags had been built into a high wall at the northern end of the track, where the water was pouring in. They had little effect.

By afternoon, Coffroth could see that the back straight away was submerged under two feet of mud. Wide canals had formed at other points on the track. The paddock was under water, as was the floor of the secretary's office under the jockeys' room. Only the stables, on a small hill above the track, were spared. Phone service was spotty but Coffroth managed to get a message through to the sports editor of the *Union*, confirming what everyone back in the city already assumed. He promised racing would resume on Saturday.

Even that looked optimistic by late afternoon. Coffroth headed to the village of Tijuana, where water levels were even higher than at the track, and saw a mother and her children clinging to a makeshift raft. They were nearing safety when the youngest child, a baby, slipped off the bucking platform into the water. As it slowly drifted away, the mother screamed and jumped in. She couldn't swim. The other children watched as she grabbed the baby with one arm and disappeared under the water. Coffroth and his racing chief, John Kelly, watched in mute horror.

"She didn't have a chance on earth to rescue the kid," Coffroth said later, "but so great was her mother love that she didn't even stop to consider that. I will never forget the sight of that poor mother leaping into the raging waters to save her child."

By nightfall, groups of refugees huddled in blankets on the slopes above the river. Only Max Kastner remained marooned. A German emigrant, Kastner lived with his wife and sister in one of the larger, two-story houses on Smythe Avenue. When he had first arrived in San Ysidro, the house had stood on lower land. Kastner moved it a few hundred yards up the slope section by section.

The women spent the day shifting furniture and belongings upstairs while Kastner moved his livestock. By now the stack reached to the attic, and Kastner had moved all the animals except a mule.

The family ignored the rescue parties' warnings.

"They kept hollering to them on a horn for them to come out," said James Russell Johnson. "But he said 'no, he wasn't afraid, he was going to stay there.' "

But as the light faded, panic set in. With only the light from the kerosene lamps on the shores to guide them, the two women waded into the water until they were breast deep. They then climbed onto a skiff that was sent out to collect them. The boat was closing in on the shore when it hit a submerged post or tree stump and capsized.

The women could not swim. For a few moments, all was confusion. The winds distorted and displaced their cries for help. Frantic strands of lamplight flickered across the water. Max Kastner crossed the river frantically on his mule. By the time he reached dry land, any trace of the women had been swept toward the ocean.

The search the following morning proved fruitless. It was weeks before the women were discovered. "Somebody discovered a foot sticking up from the ground," said James Russell Johnson. "They found the remains of the women in a clump of willow where the water had washed sand and stuff over them."

FORECAST

Federal Building, Tuesday, January 18, 1916

No local forecast for Wednesday.

—San Diego Weather Bureau

DEPRESSING

[San Diego, Wednesday, January 19, 1916]

ose Dysart stared briefly at the blank page of her diary before giving up on finding a way to break the monotonous tone it had adopted these past few days. Her pen almost wrote the opening sentence itself: "Rain, more rain."

Life at the house on Coronado was beginning to take on the air of a siege. There had been no mail in days and the local store had introduced milk rationing. Rose was a great believer in milk as the key to a healthy diet, especially for her mother, and had already spoken to the doctor about it. "The Dr. said to take some beef tea with it," she wrote.

Aware of the sickness in the house, the neighbors rallied around. "Mrs. Foster sent mother some orange marmalade in glasses," Rose wrote in her diary. But there was no lifting her mother's mood, it seemed. "She is very much depressed," wrote Rose. "This weather is very depressing."

The *San Diego Union* preferred another description of the rain, and the water it was delivering to the area. "Almost unbelievable," it called the latest figures from the statistician James Muirhead's office.

In all, the city's water system held 7.6 billion gallons more than it did on the previous Friday morning. Muirhead believed this exceeded the previous highest figure by "nearly 700 per cent." He released two sets of figures: one for the thirty-two hours between 7:00 A.M. Monday and 3:00 P.M. Tuesday, another for the eight hours between 7:00 A.M. and 3:00 P.M. on Tuesday.

At Morena, 5.76 inches of rain had fallen in a day and a half. Morena's total supply was now greater than at any time in its history, a shade over 8.5 billion gallons. The runoff rates were the most shocking statistics of all. In the thirty-two-hour period, more than 2 billion gallons had arrived at Morena. In the eight-hour period on Tuesday, the reservoir had collected 706 million gallons. Water was pouring in at a rate of almost 90 million gallons per hour.

Morena's shape meant that, even though the water level was now just 14 feet from the spillway, it was still barely half full. The same could not be said of the city's other dams.

The *Union's* front page was devoted to the "Thundering Niagara" that was Sweetwater Dam. A reporter and photographer from the paper had made their way up to the dam, where they spoke with John F. Covert, the dam's hydraulic engineer. When the storm began, the dam held just over 6 billion gallons of water. Now, with its 11-billion-gallon capacity met, Covert estimated that water was pouring out of the spillway at a rate of 4.5 billion gallons a day. Enough water had been impounded to keep National City and Chula Vista in fresh water for five years.

The Lower Otay Dam was also collecting water at record rates. Almost 350 million gallons had flowed in during eight hours on Tuesday. Just over 9 billion gallons were impounded. The dam held 11 billion gallons, although it had never held more than 10.5 billion. However, the water department was not expecting that level to be reached. It would require the rain to fall at the same freakish rate for another twenty-four hours or so. With the storm abating, that seemed unlikely.

Nine days after his weather factory had been praised for its miraculous abilities, Herbert Nimmo was forced to admit that he didn't have a clue what was going on in the skies above San Diego. "It may rain some more and then it may not."

At 6:06 A.M. that morning, the Federal Building shook with the sound of thunder. Outside, a strange new storm sent down a lightning bolt that jumped from a trolley-car wire to the roof of the car itself and then to the East San Diego fire bell. The bolt provided "a brilliant pyrotechnical display" and rang the fire bell as it "had never been rung before." The new storm continued until just after 1:00 P.M. By then it had taken out almost every line of communication in the city and left the weather bureau scrambling for new information either from San Francisco or elsewhere in the bureau's network of weather stations.

"For the first time in years the local weather bureau was unable to make its own report and forecast yesterday as to what kind of weather San Diegans might expect the following day," a mildly mocking *Union* account read. The inhabitants of the "wonderful weather factory" must have felt betrayed by the change of tone. The headline read: WEATHER GUESSER PUZZLED BY FIVE DAYS OF RAINFALL.

Down at the waterfront, there was no shortage of alternative soothsayers.

Old seadog Captain Peleg Peters, was sure that a new moon on Thursday would bring clear weather. Others quoted the old saw, "With the wind before the rain, hoist your topsail up again." This proved as reliable a guide as any. The sun appeared later in the afternoon.

Around the city, the weather continued to be a mixed blessing. Many stores were cleaned out of wet-weather clothing and umbrellas. "If we had known this fellow Hatfield was going to turn on the water and throw away the key, we could have stocked up a bit," opined one salesman. "Next time that fellow starts milking the skies we are going to send a rush order to New York for a special trainload of raincoats, rubbers and umbrellas."

The Weggeman's Bootery on 5th Street was doing a brisk trade, in particular with a "good-looking Cousins Boot in fine black calf." The weatherproof shoe was, according to its advertisements, "ultra stylish" and "adapted for such weather as Mr. Hatfield brings."

Elsewhere the shortages were more serious. With all but a handful of the city's two dozen or so Chinese and Japanese market gardeners under water and the Little Landers' deliveries abandoned until further notice, there were no fresh vegetables in the city. Grocery stores were down to their last few heads of lettuce. In the city's kitchens the situation was made even worse by the water. It gushed out of the faucets a milky brown and was undrinkable unless boiled.

The rains had even hit the wedding trade. The *Sun* reported that "Kid Cupid had come a mighty poor second to J Pluvius . . . Up to noon today not a single youth or maiden had showed up for marriage licenses at the court house," its report ran. The clerk summed up the mood of the city: "This state of affairs is almost without precedent. It is due to the rains."

Few enterprises were feeling quite as unloved as the Exposition, however. After five days of rain, the once-vivid pinks, lemons, and fuchsias of the English and Montezuma gardens had merged into a muted monotone and the Dream Spanish City had taken on the air of a palace after the revolution.

Earlier in the week, with the main buildings closed and only the Spreckels Organ and the Marine and Coast Guard Artillery Bands to draw in the crowds, the cost of admission had been slashed from fifty cents to a quarter. But the long, ornate corridors echoed only with the slapping of more rain on alabaster. Since then the deserted atmosphere was heightened even more by the loss of men from both military corps, most of whom had been dispatched to help with the rescue and cleanup operations.

Exposition boss Aubrey Davidson was already panicking about his proposed reopening date of February 15. In the papers he admitted that the new foreign exhibitors were "expressing impatience" at not being able to complete their stands. The French exhibit was marooned in San Francisco.

By now the enthusiasm of New Year's Eve had completely leaked away. Much like the city as a whole, the place felt deflated.

RAIN DROPS

[San Diego, Thursday, January 20, 1916]

When Rose Dysart drew back the drapes on Thursday morning, she felt like applauding the sky. "The sun is shining and everyone looks and feels ten per cent better, I know I do," she enthused in her diary. As the weather improved, visitors dropped by the house: an aunt joined her for lunch and a neighbor, Mr. Fellow, came by and performed a valuable service by strangling a hen in the garden. All over the city, it felt like the siege was lifting.

As people ventured out, their moods were brightened further by the almost-comic strangeness of the stories flying around the city.

So many bizarre yarns were arriving in the newsroom that the *San Diego Sun* was now devoting a daily column to them: "Rain Drops." That morning it reported that beaches to the north of

Mission Bay were lined with dead abalone and lobsters. Apparently the ocean had ingested so much fresh water from the San Diego River it had become uninhabitable for shellfish.

Elsewhere, Mission Valley farmer Rex Clark claimed the flood picked up one of his enormous concrete grain silos and floated it a mile downstream. Clark's tale not only had the silo coming to rest on another of his ranches, but—and even the *Sun* had its doubts about this—"The contents of the silo were intact. None of the fodder had even spilled."

There were other good-luck stories. City Treasurer Don Stewart had found a man hanging from a tree. His trousers and undershirt were shredded, and he was gripping an envelope in his hand. When the man was finally helped down, he approached a woman on the riverbank. "He handed her the envelope and she hugged him," recalled Stewart. "Years later I heard that this envelope contained $6,000 worth of jewelry which he had gone back to save."

Others were not so fortunate. Many small businessmen and farmers distrusted banks so vehemently that they retained the old Western practice of burying their savings in holes in the ground. All over the city, desperate men were coming to terms with the fact they would never see their money again. One tavern owner claimed he had lost $50,000 in buried gold savings in Mission Valley.

Almost eighty hours after they left Los Angeles, the passengers of Monday afternoon's Santa Fe service finally arrived in San Diego—by car. The train had just crossed the bridge north of Oceanside when the crossing collapsed into the surging water beneath it. With the storm at its peak, the passengers huddled together eating the few tins of food available and terrified that the next gust of wind would cast their train into the river. "Robinson Crusoe had nothing on us," said Charles Shaw, a retired businessman on his way to San Diego from Chicago. "If I live to be as old as Methuselah I will never forget the happenings of the last few days."

Eventually the passengers were rescued by a fleet of jitneys. Even then their journey to the city took hours; every fit member was pressed into service periodically to haul their vehicles free from the mud that consumed the main road into San Diego. "I understand that San Diego is happy because she has six years' water supply," said one of the survivors on his arrival. "That's fine. But if you want to see the happiest man in San Diego just gaze on me."

Taxi drivers were rapidly establishing themselves as the heroes of the hour, none more so than Helen Margaret Bowles. Bowles was already something of a celebrity in the city. Two years earlier, her application to become San Diego's first female jitney driver had created "a sensation." She'd done so well driving solo she'd been hired by the United Stage Company on the dollar-a-trip run from El Centro to San Diego. With the extra money, she swapped her $60 Model T for a $1,000 new Dodge tourer. Her exploits in getting people north around the flood-ravaged county won her more admirers.

When the storm first broke, Bowles had been caught in Mission Valley. A car came through and told her about the bridges and road being washed away. The United Stage office at El Centro had a group of "three Hindus, a banker and a salesman" who were desperate to get back to the city. "They asked me whether I would go. I didn't know what I was getting into, so I said 'sure.' " The Hindus all had bicycles and a lot of baggage. "We were pretty crowded in that five-passenger Dodge."

The only possible route back to the city was a zigzag, first southeast along the Mountain Springs Grade via Jacumba and Dulzura, then west and north via the Coronado ferry. All the way Bowles saw cars and trucks marooned in the mudslides. But she kept moving. She recalled later:

> At one slide the men dug a trench along the side of the hill, and I had to keep the car wheels in that. I went across just hoping it would hold." The mud was all consuming. "We

had a lot of trouble with bogging down all day long, often going right down to the axles. The three Hindus were very strong and willing, and pulled like a team of mules. One time we were bogged down so deep and they pulled so hard the rope broke, and they all fell over backwards. The father's turban came off; it was full of gold pieces which scattered in the mud. That was where they carried their money.

Four days later, Bowles and her passengers eventually got back to the city. She washed the Dodge and immediately started ferrying passengers north to link up with company cars from Los Angeles. It was more of the same.

"We could drive our cars as far as Sorrento Slough, just beyond Torrey Pines. There we rowed the passengers across in a boat and used a car borrowed from a rancher to carry them up to Oceanside. We crossed the San Luis Rey River on foot, on a plank which was only about ten inches wide, and a foot above the water."

At the river crossing, Bowles saw grown men and women reduced to quivering wrecks. "The passengers would just get petrified," she remembered. "We had to tell some of them to close their eyes and put their hands on our shoulders so we could lead them across."

Down at the racetrack, Jim Coffroth was still shaking his head at the spectacle he had witnessed. He and his team had spent two days second-guessing the direction the Tijuana was going to take. It switched tack repeatedly. "Every day this river changes its course—no wonder it was named after a woman," he said. "In my short existence, I never had so much trouble, not even with some of the girls with whom I thought I was in love."

Coffroth hoped three days of sunshine would dry out the track. He was confident racing could then resume "larger and better than ever." As a precaution, he recommended that "Brother Hatfield be taken off the job."

• • •

Across the border in San Ysidro, no one knew what would become of the Little Landers.

One hundred families were homeless and essentially destitute. Their entire lives had been condensed into their well-tended plots of land. Some announced they were heading back East. One member of the community, Fannie Christy, told the *Union*, "The Little Landers are dazed. They do not yet realize that the flood has taken everything they owned." Christy had attended a meeting on Wednesday night, just after the flood. "They looked helplessly toward each other. They seemed present in body only—they seemed to be groping blindly for expressions of speech. The situation is pitiful."

William Smythe gave a speech to the Chamber of Commerce asking for help. Smythe acknowledged the mistake the victims had made in building on the river bottomlands. "Though the original plan of the colony was to group the homes entirely on the mesa, using the rich bottom lands for gardening, year after year passed without serious floods. The people finally ventured to build their homes in the lowlands," he said. "It was thought that the turning of the Cottonwood Creek by the Southern California water system would permanently change the habits of the Tijuana River."

Now, Smythe concluded, the community he founded was "fighting not merely for their homes, but for a system of life on the land which means much to the entire world." The chamber immediately resolved to raise money. Other charitable organizations were already taking collections, and a special Little Landers relief fund was established. Businessmen and ordinary citizens dug into their pockets. John Spreckels and George W. Marston, owners of the eponymous department store, each contributed $50. The Universal Brotherhood and Theosophical Society staged a charity production of *As You Like It* at the Isis Theater. The fund soon eclipsed the $1,200 mark.

At the weather bureau, Dean Blake put the final touches to the first daily weather forecast since the storm hit on Monday. The telegraph system had been patched up enough for Blake and Nimmo to make contact with other stations in the region. Their bulletin explained that the storm had been part of a system that had hit half of the West. Blake said the bureau's barometers indicated the storm area was "rapidly passing eastward." He took to the streets on his bicycle for the first time that week. The forecast for Friday predicted "fair weather."

THE SUNMAKER

[San Diego, Saturday, January 22, 1916]

For the second successive day, the sky was cloudless and the breeze bore the musty bouquet of drying lumber and concrete, earth and tarmacadam. Down at the Tijuana racetrack, Jim Coffroth was convinced the improved weather was due to Jake Holtman, the "sunmaker" he had hired to counteract the sorcery at work in the Laguna Mountains.

The sun was drying up the track at such a rate that Coffroth hoped to resume racing "Monday or Tuesday." "What Holtman already has done for the Tijuana racetrack and for the city, generally, should be highly satisfactory to all concerned," Coffroth told the reporters he had summoned from across the border, unable to suppress a grin. "Of course Holtman, like Hatfield, has not disclosed his scheme for creating the wonderful sunshine of the past few days."

Coffroth's mood was mirrored all over the city. Slowly things appeared to be returning to normal.

That morning Marston's felt confident enough to roll out an advertisement for a new season of women's chapeaus. "Come Saturday and see the abundant array of new spring hats."

At City Hall, a bacteriologist announced that San Diego's water was safe to drink again. He explained that the sludgy brown liquid that had been surging out of the city's faucets for the past days was a product of the huge amounts of silt that had come through the Lower Otay filtration plant.

Attendance at the Exposition picked up. During the worst of the rains, the board had been determined to keep the fair in the headlines no matter what. The *Union* had dutifully carried reports on its daily announcements, regardless of how trivial they appeared in the context of the events engulfing the rest of the city. BUILDINGS STAND WEATHER TEST, STRUCTURES AT EXPOSITION, ALTHOUGH TEMPORARY, UNHARMED BY WIND AND RAIN, ran the headline on Tuesday. EXPOSITION ORGAN IN PERFECT CONDITION, was the nonstory on Wednesday. The only negative report had come on Friday, when the headline read SUPERINTENDENT REPORTED RECENT RAINS HAD DONE SOME DAMAGE TO THE PARK DRIVEWAYS. The *Union* added that it was "nothing of a serious nature." With the turnstiles clicking again, there was the prospect of some real news to report.

People's minds moved from the clean up to the crucial business of reconnecting the city with the outside world and helping those hit by the floods. The Little Landers fund eclipsed the $2,000 mark.

At City Hall, Hatfield remained high on the agenda. Cornered by reporters in the corridors that morning, Terence Cosgrove confided that he had spoken to the enigma in the hills. "He would be in San Diego within ten days to collect his money," the attorney predicted.

Cosgrove confirmed there was a contract but declined to give any details about its content. Asked whether Charles would be willing to sign it, he reverted to his trademark opaqueness: "If he fills Morena, he will be willing to sign it."

ISOLATED

[Coronado, Monday, January 24]

By Monday at Coronado, the sunny optimism of the weekend had disappeared. On Saturday morning, Rose and Martha Dysart, having been closeted up for more than a week, were so desperate to feel the balmy sea breezes in the house they set about opening some windows. The air was thick with the odor of linctus, liniment and chicken broth. But they were so weak from illness that the job proved too much for them and Martha sprained a wrist. To her nursing duties that evening, Rose now added the job of tending to her sister's bandages.

To everyone's disappointment, the fine weather proved a fleeting phenomenon. By Sunday, banks of slatey cumulus clouds were stacking up once more. "The sun tried to shine," Rose lamented in her diary that evening.

It didn't bother to even make an attempt on Monday. The weather note at the head of Rose's diary page simply read "cloudy." It matched the mood of the house on what was going to be a somber day anyhow. "Father died thirteen years ago today," Rose wrote.

At the camp, the rains of the past fortnight had heightened Charles's and Paul's sense of isolation, too.

Charles, in particular, had always regarded visitors as a mixed blessing. At places like Crow's Landing, the arrival of a farmer on a horse and buggy could lift the spirits. "They'd kill a beef, you know, or a hog," Paul recalled. "And eggs! Boy, they'd bring a whole case. They were hospitable people." Mostly, however, "rubber neckers" were the bane of their existence. Once, in Texas, a crowd of three thousand people gathered around their towers as they worked. "If there are too many people it produces a nuisance," Paul recalled with understatement.

The Swensons dropped in regularly. Despite her misgivings about the brothers, Maggie often arrived with home cooking. But there was no danger of a multitude ascending to the Laguna Range—particularly not with San Diego still preoccupied with mopping up.

With the ground drying out, Charles and Paul had a rare opportunity to take part in tossing horseshoes, their only real form of exercise. The break in the weather that morning also gave them a chance to give the precipitation plant a thorough overhaul.

Charles was convinced the best results came from raising his rain stew from a "nice new bright tray." After three weeks of heating chemicals, the base of the pans on the platform were flaked, dulled, and rusting in places. He and Paul replaced them with eight new trays. They then went through their customary ritual of stacking the old trays into a compact package, digging a "great big deep hole" and leaving them to rot away in the earth. The patch of raked-over earth that marked their grave was hidden away in the cottonwoods.

In the B tent, Charles went through his inventory of chemicals. He studied the latest weather reports from the city and cast his eye over the gray green expanse of Morena. A walk down to the big gauge at the front wall confirmed his suspicion. When he saw Seth Swenson, the damkeeper repeated the news he'd already passed on to the water department. The dam had reached a level of 137 feet. The runoff in the past twenty-four hours had been 115 million gallons. Seth realized the significance of this statistic as well as Charles, perhaps even better. For the first time in its history, Morena now held more than 10 billion gallons of water.

By afternoon, his barometer was registering new drops in pressure and the last wash of blue was fading from the sky. Once more the horizon was sheathed in gray.

Back up on the tower platform, Charles's gleaming new trays were soon dispatching their first pungent payload.

REAL SAN DIEGO WEATHER

[San Diego, Wednesday, January 26, 1916]

After an early supper, Seymour Tulloch, his wife, and two daughters set off from their home at 2243 Front Street on the short walk to the Broadway Cinema. The Tullochs were looking forward to seeing Mary Pickford's new film, *The Foundling*, but were anticipating the stroll almost as much. After seemingly endless days of rain, it was good to sample some sunshine and to chat with familiar faces on the bustling early-evening sidewalks.

Seymour Tulloch was the city's deputy treasurer. He liked the fact that his job kept him, as he put it, "at the center of news." All sorts of faces, from city officials to bank-runners passed through his office, exchanging snippets of information and gossip as they did so. The headquarters of the U.S. Naval Reserves were there, too. So as Tulloch chatted with acquaintances he did so with some authority. He told people about the progress being made on repairing the railroads and the telegraph and long-distance wires. He mentioned that the steamers were keeping up an irregular mail and passenger service and the car service from Los Angeles was getting through via a ferry over the river at Del Mar. He explained how the relief effort was being helped by the spell of better weather.

Like most people, Seymour Tulloch was sure "the storm was over and the worst had passed . . . this is like our real San Diego weather again."

At 7:00 P.M. the Tullochs slid into their seats at the cinema, eager to renew their love affair with "the world's sweetheart." An hour or so later, as they emerged from the movie, the depressingly familiar sight that greeted them dulled their mood.

As Tulloch took his wife and daughter's hands, he heard the sounds of doors rattling and slamming, telegraph wires humming. On Broadway, he saw lights stretched across the street near the Exposition information booth swaying wildly in the wind, their reflection illuminating the rippling water coursing down the street. The effect was eerie.

The walk back home was chaotic. What had, a few hours earlier, been an enjoyable exercise was once more transformed into a drenching slog. Umbrellas turned inside out and broke loose. The journey was conducted in disgusted silence.

The rain's return wasn't entirely unexpected. In its forecast that morning, the weather bureau had warned: "Unsettled tonight and Thursday." After the drama of the last seven days, however, Herbert Nimmo felt the need to reassure people. "He did not expect another storm so severe as that of last week," the *Union* reported that morning, "but that J Pluvius would nevertheless drop some slight tokens on San Diego."

The warning was accompanied by pinches of humor. The front page of that morning's *Union* featured a large cartoon by W. C. Baker, in which a straw-hatted farmer chased "Jupiter Pluvius" Hatfield "toward the bay." An automobile-parts store placed an advertisement in the morning's *Sun*: "Hatfield is making more slick roads. Get those anti-skid chains."

160

"JUPITER PLUVIUS" HATFIELD WOULD EVEN GET "HIS" FROM THE
FARMER NOW — IF HE COULD BE "GOT AT!"

A Wanted Man. A cartoonist shows a farmer chasing "Jupiter Pluvius" Hatfield
"towards the bay." *San Diego Union,* January 26, 1916.

As the evening wore on, however, the mood in the Federal
Building began to change. The rains had begun at around 7:30
P.M. The accompanying winds were coming from the southwest,
the bureau's blind spot, and were gusting at high speeds. Nimmo
admitted that "several telegraphic reports from the northwestern
part of the country were missing." This was "making it difficult
for the local weather force to tell the exact force or location of
the storm center." Nimmo and Blake spent the night troubled by
the lack of certainty.

They were not alone in their thoughts.

Back in his bed in the city, Seymour Tulloch lay awake listening to the gathering tumult. "As the night passed the storm
continued and seemed to increase in violence," he wrote later, in
his regular Sunday letter to his daughter Marjorie.

As he listened to the unnatural weather, he was filled with a
dread that it was not merely undoing the good work of the past
few days.

To Dorothy Clark Schmid, the sounds coming from the valleys
and creeks below the family homestead in the hamlet of Dulzura

suggested the end of the world. She knew the mountain slopes were so saturated that any rain was going to loosen more earth and rock from the mountainsides.

The surges of water proved too much for the flume connecting Morena to the Barrett Reservoir. The conduit broke and the resulting torrent washed out the Campo road five hundred yards below the point where it crossed the Cottonwood.

The intensity of the storm was terrifying. "The noise from the boulders as they crashed by was terrific and there were intermittent peals of sound which may have been from landslides or thunder," she said. The display of light visible through the windows, was, if anything, even more unsettling. "The dark sky would seem to light up now and then although there were no flashes of lightning as in a thunder storm."

PART IV

The Cataclysm [January 27–30, 1916]

Breached. The Sweetwater Dam, San Diego, Thursday, January 27, 1916. (San Diego Historical Society)

ONE WILD SCENE

[San Diego, Thursday Morning, January 27, 1916]

Shortly after 5:00 A.M. a cacophony of bells, whistles, and fire-engine sirens summoned a section of downtown San Diego from its sleep. The alarms were directed at the residents of a grid of streets on the steep hill below the southern end of Balboa Park and were accompanied by male voices, distorted and enlarged by megaphones. As they shook themselves awake, people realized they were being told to gather their belongings. They were being ordered to evacuate.

A team of workers had been monitoring one of the city's small "feeder" dams, in Switzer Canyon near 20th and B streets, all night. The concrete dam at the southern end of Balboa Park was intended to gather the park's water and feeding it out to the Bay via a five-foot cement conduit. By 4:30 A.M., however, the flume could not cope with the volumes of water coursing in. The dam began to overflow at 5:00 A.M.

Rather than risk the whole dam bursting, a team of engineers made the decision to dynamite the western end of the dam and allow the water to flood out more slowly. Teams ran down into the streets below to warn people. The explosion went off around 7:30 A.M.

Daisy Abell was preparing her children for school when she heard her daughter shouting. The girl had looked out of their home on 15th Street, between I and J streets, to see a surging tide of water heading toward the house. The yard was filling rapidly with water and soon they would be encircled.

Daisy took the children and ran off to use the phone at a nearby lumberyard to call her husband. By the time she got back, a neighbor had backed a horse and buggy into her front yard and was helping to rescue their belongings.

Daisy noticed that the water lapping three to four feet up her walls was now glazed with thick oil. The rising tide had broken through the stilts holding the local laundry's fuel tanks. She fled to her daughter's boyfriend's home on higher ground on Market Street. On her way she glanced down the adjoining streets. The brunt had been taken by houses on 14th, 15th, 16th, and 17th streets. The most incredible sights lay on 16th Street. Two houses, numbers 1019 and 1033, had been flipped onto their sides by the tidal wave. "Everything was ruined," she remembered.

The damage inflicted on her own home was so bad that it would be four months before her husband would allow her to see it again.

On the third floor of the Federal Building, the weathermen's sense of mild alarm was hardening into something far more unsettling. Blake and Nimmo's desks were covered with a mass of statistics gathered by the tripleograph overnight and a blizzard of wire reports from bureaus around the nation.

Back in Washington, the bureau concluded that the entire

Pacific Coast was being battered by a storm. The front's progress east was being blocked by an enormous area of high pressure in the northwest. The high was so intense that it had produced temperatures of -54°F in Havre, Montana. The atmospheric logjam meant the storm was effectively stuck over Southern California and San Diego, where rain was falling harder than anywhere else in the United States.

The high wind worried the bureau even more. Again the figures were unprecedented. At around 4:30 that morning, the anemometer had recorded the strongest winds the city had ever seen. For a five-minute period the sustained winds reached 54 miles per hour, with even stronger gusts. For a one-minute period it reached 62 miles per hour. According to the strict rules of the weather bureau, winds needed to blow for at least five minutes to be considered a record. The previous strongest wind was 45 miles per hour in February 1914. But of even greater concern was the wind's direction. It was coming in from the bureau's "blind spot," the south and southwest.

So much water was tumbling down the steep grades of 15th and 16th streets that Shelley Higgins had to take refuge on a horse-drawn fire truck. Making the same journey along G Street the previous night, the attorney had been able to roll up his pants and make it home barefoot. But even that was impossible today. Downtown San Diego had been transformed into a miniature Venice. On Broadway, the water was five feet deep.

On board the fire engine, Higgins heard that distress calls were coming in from Tijuana in the south to Fallbrook in the north. Minutes later, in the dry warmth of his office, the reports arriving on his desk confirmed the firemen's claims that the entire county was "saturated, bogged down, washed out, inundated and isolated."

With the Switzer Canyon Dam dealt with, the main cause for concern now was the city's larger dams: Morena, Sweetwater, and the Lower Otay.

FORECAST:-- RAIN TONIGHT AND FRIDAY

Extra   FULL LEASED WIRE SERVICE OF UNITED PRESS ASSOCIATIONS
The San Diego Sun   **Extra**

THIRTY-FIFTH YEAR.   WHOLE NO. 10,712.   THURSDAY, JANUARY 27, 1916.   SAN DIEGO, CALIFORNIA.

DYNAMITE DAM IN PARK; FIGHT TO SAVE CITY BRIDGE

Explosive News. San Diego learns of the destruction of the Switzer Dam. *San Diego Sun*, Thursday, January 27, 1916.

The latest statistics were made public in that day's *Union*. Morena's water level had risen by 17.5 feet in the ten days between January 14 and 24. Lower Otay had risen even more—by 27.25 feet. Of course, Muirhead's figures were already out of date.

That morning Lower Otay was rising at the rate of almost one foot an hour. City Manager Fred Lockwood had called in the original engineers. Poring over the plans, they assured him the dam was safe. But Lockwood wasn't prepared to take the risk.

Since Wednesday morning, the city's main telephone and telegraph companies were reporting new ruptures in the lines out of the city. Newly raised poles were flattened by the wind. The lines to Los Angeles in the north were already lost and lines to the south were erratic at best.

Lockwood dispatched a team of horsemen to the valley with instructions to order evacuation to higher ground.

In Mission Valley, railway and city workers were doing all they could to stave off the surging tide of the San Diego River. The river had swollen overnight and the Old Town bridge was in jeopardy. Once again the mile-wide valley was submerged across its entire length. The wind was driving the flood forward. From the

168

heights above the valley, the undulating water resembled the back of some strange sea creature moving slowly oceanward. From the safety of their homes on the bluffs, people watched the water perform a reprise of the surreal events of the previous week.

At 4:00 P.M. a crack appeared in the midsection of the bridge. The workers were called off immediately. Within moments one of the center arches sagged, doubled up, and slowly toppled into the river. A few minutes later, the northern section of the bridge collapsed. The current turned it around as if it were a floating tree branch. The vast concrete construction was carried twenty feet downstream.

"The cheaply-constructed dirt dyke was saved but the expensive bridge structure was sacrificed," Walter Bellon of the health department wrote later. "A few sticks of dynamite well placed in the dirt dyke would have saved the bridge and most of the road. This was a successful blunder."

When the order to abandon the bridge was given, one member of the salvage team, Edwin Thill, had run to the northern side. The bridge soon collapsed behind him. Thill needed to get back to the southern side of the river, so he headed to the Santa Fe railway bridge a few hundred yards away.

With their bridge also jeopardized, officials from the railway had filled the length of the crossing with heavily loaded freight cars. Thill was left stranded on the northern bank. Ninety minutes after the first bridge collapsed, the railway bridge went, too. The cars were swept toward Mission Bay with the rest of the city's debris. Thill remained stranded. He could not have felt alone; all over the county, one hundred lesser bridges had already been swept away.

By late afternoon John Covert had calculated that the amount of water coming into Sweetwater Dam was greater than that he could release through the dam's spillways and blow-off valves. Water had reached the rim of the dam at 2:20 P.M. By 4:30, a wall of water more than three feet deep was flowing over the rim.

"Sacrificed." San Diegans survey the damage to the Old Town Bridge in the aftermath of the flood. (San Diego Historical Society)

At the north end of the dam there was an earth-filled dike; the water was eating this away, too. "The water washed away this fill, broke the concrete-core wall, and cut a by-pass around the dam," Covert later reported. The question now was whether the dam would be able to withhold the force. When one of the dam workers, John Boal, rang the *Union* to raise the alarm, his voice was grave. Boal was asked whether the dam was in danger of collapsing completely. "I fear it may," he replied sadly.

With phone lines failing all the time, an odd peace descended on City Hall. At his desk, Seymour Tulloch, the deputy treasurer, struggled to concentrate on the housekeeping task before him that week, processing the month's invoices so they could be paid at the end of the week. "It was almost impossible to work," he wrote later.

News of the Switzer Dam break had come in early. Then, from the U.S. Naval Reserves office in the same building, he had heard of men being dispatched to Mission Valley to deal with the threat to the city's main bridge at Old Town. Other snippets of news drifted in through the day: people living on higher ground in Brooklyn Heights and South Park were cut off from the city; water was flowing over the National City dike; key bridges had gone out north and south of the city.

Tulloch called his wife Didi at home to break the news now dawning on him. "San Diego is all cut off by transportation from the outside world, except by ships," he told her.

At 4:00 P.M. he decided to leave for the day. He wanted to see the destruction for himself and headed for Mission Hill Gardens, the highest vantage point he knew.

Within minutes he was soaked to the skin. The storm seemed to be gaining power by the hour. Gusts of wind were casting roof tiles into the air like autumn leaves. There were few figures on the streets. Those who braved it leaned into the wind.

He caught one of the few streetcars running up as far as Jack Daw Street on Mission Hill. From there he dropped his shoulder into the teeth of the storm and walked a few blocks to a point where he could see the valley. The scene that greeted him beggared belief. "It was one whirling mass of angry waters from bluff to bluff," he wrote later. "The sky was wet and lowering with dripping storm clouds flying low, and the mists and fogs drifted like curtains across the far ends. It was certainly one wild scene of desolation, nature's relentlessness, and man's weakness."

Tulloch struggled to keep upright. Standing up straight was impossible, so he took refuge in the lee of a large house. He was talking to its owner when he noticed a farmhouse floating loose, "gradually swinging around on its foundation like a steamer warping at a dock." He watched in awe as it straightened up. "Finally it got its head down stream and off it started, standing almost upright in the flood. After it had gone some distance the kitchen all but broke off and—being lighter—said goodbye, and raced off on its own account."

Soon afterward he saw another house go by, this time out in

the middle of the water, a full quarter-mile away from him. He saw a man walking on its flat roof. "He was trying for help for himself and a boy within." Tulloch was powerless to help from such a distance. They disappeared from view in moments.

Tulloch started home haunted by the image of the father and son. It stayed with him long after he had entered the warmth of his living room.

In the late afternoon, less than a mile apart from each other, Charles Hatfield and Seth Swenson looked out over the rippling gray expanse of Morena Lake. The two men harbored divergent emotions, but one common, recurring thought. Neither could quite believe what he was witnessing.

The skies had broken open again that morning with an intensity that had been shocking. Within minutes the saturated earth was virtually boiling with excess runoff. For Charles it was a sight to send his spirits soaring. As a young man, his fascination with the weather had been fired by travelers' tales of tropical rains so powerful they could knock fish unconscious and drown birds in the trees. He never imagined he would see rain capable of such things. If it kept up, the vast reservoir would be filled within days—or less.

Charles had not acted on Fred Binney's warning about the lack of a contract. He reasoned that the matter was academic until he filled Morena, and no one could reasonably blame him. Morena had never been remotely near full. Who could deny him his right to the $10,000 now?

Seth Swenson's mind was preoccupied with more disturbing calculations and a darker question: How much more water could Morena contain safely?

At 7:00 A.M. the walk along the rim of the dam had been a precarious high-wire act in the wind. But Seth was able to read the gauges and relay his report to the water department. Runoff was still building at a phenomenal rate: 169 million gallons in the last twenty-four hours. The dam now held more than 10 billion gallons.

If he had not been so worried, he might have been able to celebrate the fact.

The keeper paced the dam wall all morning and was away from the phone when George Cromwell, the city's engineer, rang the cottage. Maggie spoke to Cromwell and took down his instructions with care. Cromwell told her more rain was expected but that the city needed every drop. He made it clear that Seth should not open the spillways unless the dam was ready to overflow.

By the time he received the message, Seth's concerns were growing more acute. The dense layering of scrub, rock, and trees on the surrounding slopes had always been Morena's protection against sudden bursts of runoff. Today the slopes were turned into raging watercourses. By afternoon the water level was rising at 2 feet per hour. Waves were chopping into the dam wall less than 20 feet from the top. Seth didn't need precise figures; he knew instinctively that if the rain persisted Morena would be full within twelve hours. Perhaps sooner.

He was due to call back with his usual 7:00 P.M. reading. The instructions that afternoon could not have come from a higher level, so his argument for opening the spillways would have to be good. In his mind he practiced the speech he would give. Then—sometime in the afternoon—the wind tore down the phone lines in the valley below the cottage.

At the Sweetwater Dam, a trio of engineers—John Boal, John Covert, and P. D. Mahoney—were convinced they had witnessed a minor miracle.

The breach on the southern side of the dam hadn't affected the water level of the reservoir significantly. Although water was surging out at a rate of millions of gallons a minute, the runoff entering the dam was such that the water level dropped by only an inch or two at most.

The trio saw that the water had begun to erode an earth-filled dike at the north side of the dam. Like the southern breach, it gave way slowly at first and then surrendered suddenly. Again they watched helplessly and wondered if this would finally undermine the dam.

But the second break acted as a release valve. "The water poured out in tremendous quantities and seemed to relieve the pressure on the remainder of the cement work," Boal said. He stuck around for an hour before he was convinced the dam was going to hold. "The dam seemed to be standing the terrific strain splendidly," he told the water department before the lines went dead.

The relief felt at City Hall was immense but short-lived.

Just before 5:00 P.M. supervisor Rudolph Wueste set off to complete the walk back across the parapet of the Lower Otay Dam. The situation had been deteriorating all day. By late morning it was clear that the volume of runoff was going to overwhelm the structure. Another engineer wrote later: "By noon, the water had risen so high that Mr. Wueste . . . deemed it advisable to open the outlet gate. This failed to check the rise, and it was realized that the dam would probably be overtopped before evening. Men were accordingly dispatched to warn residents in the valley to move to higher ground."

At around 4:00 P.M., Wueste had walked across the dam from north to south. Half an hour later, he saw the first trickle of water lapping over the rim. By the time he headed back to the northern side of the dam, the trickle had turned into a widening stream. He had to jump across it. As he crossed, Wueste saw that the water was carving its way into the two feet of earth and gravel that lay on top of the heavier, coarser rock. Soon after he reached the other side, most of the two-foot topping had been eaten away.

From his vantage point at the northern end, Roy Silent saw water running down the outside face of the dam. A moment later, Silent saw "several spouts or small streams of water on the lower face of the dam, in one instance loosening a large boulder which rolled down. From this time on, the destruction was very rapid." At exactly 5:05 P.M., the dam gave way. "The tension was so great that the steel diaphragm tore from the top at the center, and the dam opened outward like a pair of gates."

Wueste later said it was like watching a mountain of sugar slowly dissolving. The sound it made was also strange. It was a metallic banging, as if some Brobdingnagian blacksmith was at work at his anvil. He soon saw what it was.

The metal sheet that Elisha Babcock, the dam's builder, had improvised at the heart of the dam had been ripped loose and left flapping. Millions of tons of water were pounding into and past it. After a brief time, however, the banging ceased. Silent and Wueste watched as the sheet merged into the forty-foot wall of water that was plunging into the valley below them.

ALL DEAD

[Otay Valley, Thursday Evening, January 27, 1916]

M anuel Daneri was a stern patriarch, a man possessed, so his family said, of a temper as fiery as his head of thick red hair. When one of his two daughters, Flora, ran off with a hired hand, he disowned her and forbade anyone in the family from contacting her. At her first dinner with the family, his daughter-in-law Aurelia de Bincenzi made a friendly remark about what a handsome father-in-law she had acquired. The look he gave her was chilling. "I knew I had made a mistake. He was very aristocratic and strict."

No one could argue that his tyranny had not borne fruit. The wines and brandies he produced at his nine-hundred-acre winery in the Otay Valley and sold in his store beneath the Lincoln Hotel on Fifth Street ended up on San Diego's grandest dinner tables. Nor could anyone deny his philanthropy. He had found jobs for scores of nephews and nieces from the poorer branch of the family in San Francisco. In the village of Otay, Daneri had built the valley's only schoolhouse. He also allowed a community of Japanese market gardeners to work the fields at the lower end of his domain.

Daneri's mood had been dark all day Thursday. He didn't appreciate people telling him how to run his business and he certainly didn't enjoy being told to evacuate his home.

Shelley Higgins had been at the receiving end of Daneri's ire when he called from City Hall in the morning. The attorney recalled, "He scoffed at my fears, and said he was high enough not to be touched if the dinky little dam did bust."

Late in the afternoon, Daneri was being told to move to his face, this time by Bill Gallagher, the water department's "pipe walker."

Gallagher was one of four men dispatched by Rudolph Wueste, superintendent of the city impounding system, that morning. Gallagher set off on horseback, working his way up the valley in the driving rain, warning every home of the threat of the Otay's breaking. His warning was greeted with a mixture of gratitude, skepticism, and bafflement. The Japanese community spoke poor English and, failing to grasp the urgency of Gallagher's warning, had stayed put.

By the time he reached the Daneris' home around 5:00 P.M., Gallagher was ready to drop. He hadn't eaten since first thing that morning. The Daneri family's cook of thirty-six years, Rosa Mosto, was preparing the evening meal. She set an extra place for him alongside her brother Joe and other longtime Daneri workers, Carlo Evallo, Ramone Mehia, and Carlo Bega.

It was around 5:30 P.M. when Manuel's wife appeared at the door of the dining room and shouted for her husband to join the dinner table. Bill Gallagher's warnings had unsettled her; she was anxious to eat the evening meal and move out for the night.

Manuel had gone up the hill to his wine cellar in search of a bottle or two to accompany the meal. As he emerged, he heard a low rumbling farther up the valley. He was one step from the door of his house when he saw a sheet of water coming through a side window.

He reacted instinctively and jumped toward his wife. He pulled her out of the house, shouting as they went. They ran uphill into the olive grove above the house. In the fading light it wasn't easy to see, but the colossal roar and the intermittent explosions they heard behind them told the story.

The collapse of the Lower Otay Dam had unleashed a killing force.

A single cubic yard of water weighs roughly 1,500 pounds. At the time it gave way, Lower Otay contained 10 billion gallons of water and it is safe to guess the headwall of the tidal wave would have weighed around 1,500 tons. Its momentum would have generated a power in multiple of this.

Sixteen years earlier, in 1900, the tidal wave that accompanied the great hurricane in Galveston was believed to have generated 1,000 tons of force. It was powerful enough to destroy artillery emplacements that were designed to withstand Spanish bombardments. The wave that was now released into the narrow Otay Valley carried a comparable force. Its twelve-mile journey to San Diego Bay would take only forty-eight minutes. During that time, it was not going to encounter anything remotely as resilient as gunnery emplacements.

George Laustaulett was in his barn milking with his son. The lowing of the cows had drowned out the booming in the valley above. Forty feet of water was about to bear down on them when his son happened to look up and out through the barn door. "Here it comes, dad," he shouted. The wave cut through the barn and swept everything with it. Father and son stayed close enough to guide each other to a grove of large trees farther down the valley. Both caught a low branch, then clambered up to safety.

The six miles of valley that lay between the winery and the

bay contained two dozen homes. Only one—belonging to the Hulett family—survived.

Howard Banks owned the general store on Otay's main street. The rising waters had consumed it that afternoon and all that remained of his $8,000 stock of groceries were a case of peas and a wheel of cheese. Before the dam burst he had taken heed of the warnings and set off to persuade others to move to higher ground. Many refused to budge. John Dube, an infirm old-timer, was in bed and couldn't be moved anyway, his wife Margaret said.

Now, with the dam gone, all he could do was run along the hillside and watch. At one point he saw a husband and wife struggling in the raging water. He told his wife about it later. "The poor husband had a hold of his wife's long black hair with one hand and was struggling against the rampaging water, trying to reach an embankment," she recalled. "Nobody ever saw them again."

At the peak of its power, passing through Palm City, the wave found the new concrete-and-steel railway embankment of the San Diego & Arizona Line directly in its path. By now its force was enhanced by the debris it had accumulated on the way down. "The seething wave, bearing before it spars of wood, roofs of houses, trees, and rubbish, hit the railroad embankment with a smash," said one witness. "The waters towered what seemed to be a hundred feet in the air." Most witnesses expected the eighty-foot-high embankment to check the wave's progress. It did, but only for the few seconds it took for the irresistible force to seek out the weak spots within the newest obstruction. "It hesitated there, that was all, then it headed on to the sea."

Just before 6:00 P.M., out on the Coronado side of San Diego Bay, the steamship *Cyprus* was riding out the storm. The ship's anchor chain groaned and on deck, every joint creaked.

Suddenly, through the darkness and horizontal rain, the men on the bridge were aware of a massive shape looming silently toward them. Before they could take evasive action, it was gliding past the ship's stern. The *Cyprus's* lights illuminated the mass for a few seconds. As it did so, the crew heard the sound of cattle. The cows were clinging to what looked like a section of a bridge. It was the most surreal thing anyone had ever seen.

Manuel Daneri and his wife scrambled out of the valley toward the home of their daughter, Ella, and her husband, John Schroeder.

At the Schroeders, they were amazed to find their son John waiting. He'd had a presentiment and headed up along the railway line with a reporter from the *San Diego Union*.

His mother collapsed, weeping, into his arms.

"It's no use," she sobbed. "Joe is dead. Rosa is dead. They're all dead. Our clothes are all we have left. . . ."

Seth Swenson made up his mind at midnight. The rain was still tumultuous, and the threat to the dam's structure was unmistakable.

By now the water was within touching distance of the two-foot concrete coping that sat on top of the dam wall. The coping had been added more as a guardrail than part of the dam itself. Swenson knew it could not contain such vast weights of water. He knew he could not delay the water any longer.

Out on the lake, it was an effort to row into the face of the wind. When he reached the outlet tower, he climbed up the outside and eased himself into the opening at the top of the funnel. Even by the light of the oil lantern, the long drop below him was a pitch-black void. The tower contained five valves. The immense concrete tube warped the wind into banshee wails as he picked his way down the ladder. It was 1:30 A.M. before he reached the first outlet at 99.5 feet. He maintained them regularly, but had never needed to use them. After a struggle, the wheels groaned, then loosened.

For a time he listened in the semidarkness. Eventually, somewhere far below him, he heard a sonorous rumble. He knew that deep in the gorge beneath the dam, millions of gallons of water were now surging loose. But he also knew that millions of gallons more were continuing to pour in. It would be the longest night of his life. He asked himself the same questions over and over: Had he acted in time? Had he done enough?

AFTERMATH

[Friday, January 28, 1916]

At daybreak, Charles and Paul picked their way down the muddy slope beneath their camp, drawn by the thunderous rumbling that had been coming from the direction of the dam most of the night. The sight that greeted them took their breath away. "The water was going over four feet deep," Paul recalled. "Like Niagara Falls."

As he watched the foaming water fall into the valley, Seth Swenson felt only relief. Sleep had been an impossibility until he knew the dam was safe. By first light he saw the torrent flowing through the spillways. The rains over the mountain seemed to be easing, but he knew that millions of gallons of runoff still had to come in. It would be a battle to stabilize the dam. The water level was just five inches below the top of the coping. Five inches had separated Morena, the valley below, and San Diego itself from disaster.

At 7:00 A.M. Swenson went to the gauge and wrote down a figure he never believed possible: 150.5 feet. The dam had taken in almost 5 billion gallons since the previous morning. Morena reservoir now held 15.45 billion gallons of water. It was full to the brim.

Dawn in San Diego drew the curious out of their homes and into a landscape of surreal new sights.

Through the windows of his home on 12th Street, Shelley Higgins looked out to see herds of displaced and distressed animals wandering the otherwise-deserted downtown streets. In the pale light Higgins made out "cattle, horses, mules, sheep—even goats—loose in our streets."

Robert Holmes, an Englishman, recently arrived in the city, instinctively headed for the bay and met a man staggering down the road in a drunken stupor. "I wondered where he got the booze," Holmes remarked. At the shore he saw that the giant vats from the Daneri winery had finally run aground. The scene on the beach had the flavor of burlesque, peopled with drunks, over-laden looters, and children reveling in the strange discoveries they were making.

As he walked the beach, Holmes saw it was littered with the bloated carcasses of farm animals: cows, horses, and hogs. "And thousands of snakes. I never saw so many snakes in my life as what I saw swimming around in the bay." Back in the city, children were already selling them at 50 cents apiece.

City Treasurer Don Stewart was making grimmer discoveries.

Stewart was also a naval reservist and took to the water in a skiff. Easing his way through the sludge brown waters, he saw a delta of debris, several hundred yards wide, spewed out on to the shore. Stewart quickly realized this was where Lower Otay's wall of mud and water had reached the end of its journey. Amongst the clocks, windmill towers, roof sections, pianos, and chicken coops, he recognized the metallic glint of the sheet core of the Otay Dam. Elisha Babcock's bright idea had arrived at its journey's end crumpled up like a ball of tinfoil.

Stewart saw the waters farther down the bay were dotted with other boats. They were filled with Japanese farmers, lost in their grim-faced search for their dead. He left them to their task.

Nearby, at the salt vats off Palm Avenue, a local resident named Mary Addis led another search party. "We saw arms and legs sticking up where the dead had come down," Addis recalled.

Eventually two men, Bill Wolf and Clarence Harris, waded into the thigh-deep mud. "The force of the water was so great it had taken off all their clothes except their shoes," recalled Harris, an eighteen-year-old serving in the Army Air Service on the Mexican border.

Wolf and Harris found it hard to lever the corpses loose, but finally hauled the dead back to drier ground, where a coroner was waiting. "Every bone was broken," Harris said. "When we tried to pick them up they were just as limp as beef."

The bodies turned out to be Bill Gallagher, Rosa Mosta, and the other victims of the Daneri disaster.

To his amazement, Howard Banks found one of the men he had failed to remove from his home the previous day. He was still sitting in his chair, a big tree lodged across his lap, and every stitch of his clothing torn away. He was blue with cold. He died a month later.

The Dubes were found in the bay. Margaret was floating dead in the water. John Dube was found lying dead, yet peaceful in his nightclothes under the covers of his bed. The wave had carried the bed all the way to the shore intact.

At 7:00 A.M., Dorothy Clark Schmid's rain gauge at Dulzura had picked up 6.9 inches of rain in twenty-four hours. Some years it didn't rain much more than 5 inches during the entire season. The Schmid family stepped out into the thin morning light, apprehensive at what they would find.

It did not take them long to register the scale of the destruction. "As the low heavy clouds lifted we could see the great and small landslides on the mountains looking as though some great beast had clawed them," Dorothy said.

As they picked their way through the landscape, familiar sights had been transformed.

The once perennially green meadow at the Harvey Ranch was cut through and ruined. Below Bratton Valley the road wound down through a delightful fern-filled dell called "the Nest" where the damage was grievous and the road over which the ranchers had slaved for years was completely obliterated.

The surface soil simply slipped away from the mountains in terrible rents. The greatest slide, acres in extent, was on the north side of Lyons Peak where boulders big as houses thundered down the mountain crushing oak trees to a pulp.

Runoff from Otay Mountain had surged into Sycamore Canyon, while the excess water from the hills above Bratton Valley had filled Pringle Canyon. The waves pouring down both had filled Dulzura Creek. Dorothy recalled, "The stream, which was normally a swift brook in the rainy season, became a muddy torrent bearing great live oaks on its crest and sweeping out orchard trees along with all the bridges and their approaches. One of Mr. Hagenbuck's barns was carried away and his wagon rolled gaily on the tide with all wheels spinning."

The Cottonwood Valley had also taken "a terrible punishment with trees and houses and stock swept away." Dorothy knew an old settler, Mrs. Bloch, who lived at the foot of the old grade road to Cottonwood Valley. "Mrs. Bloch . . . saw the homestead she had created with her own hands all but covered with debris from above."

Schmid met a relative, Louis Harvey. Harvey knew the history of the area's water system—and the Lower Otay Dam in particular. Throughout the storm he told his sons that the dam couldn't hold. That morning he took his boys to a lookout point where they could see down into the Otay Valley. "There in the sunlight, which was breaking through the clouds, they saw the yellow mud where the dam had been."

By the end of the day, she was sure of one thing: "The heartbreaks can never be estimated in monetary value."

Back in his office at City Hall, Seymour Tulloch heard that the father and son he had watched floating down Mission Valley the previous evening had been rescued by the U.S. Navy at 2:00 A.M. It was one of the few pieces of good news flowing into the council offices.

It didn't help that the information coming in was slow and confused. With the lines to the Otay Valley down, the *Union* offices had been telling callers that the dam was safe. DAMS HOLDING AGAINST GREAT FLOODS AS WIRES GO: CITY SUPPLY ALL RIGHT was its main headline on that morning's front page.

First word of Otay's collapse came from F. E. Baird, one of the dam workers, who had evacuated a length of ranches below the dam before he was hit by the edge of the wave. He somehow scrambled his way free before being caught up completely. "It was a terrible sight. Trees were swept away like twigs. Nothing could have stood in the path of that seething, twisting, roaring wall of water."

Men who had been declared dead walked into their living rooms as if resurrected from the grave. Deputy U.S. Marshal William Carse turned up at his home at Coronado bleeding, speechless, and "more dead than alive" after walking the pipeline up toward the Daneri winery. An Otay farmer named Loper, who had been presumed dead after his house was seen being smashed to pieces against a bridge, turned up with the most vivid survival tale. Baird and another "pipewalker" named Osborn had warned him to clear out. He was changing his clothes and packing a bag when "a crash of trees in the nearby grove told me the waters had come. The roar became deafening. The first wave struck me at the knees as I sped for the hills, the second bowled me over, and fighting half on my feet half off, I groped in the darkness. A straw sack came along and swamped me, a barbed wire fence fastened itself upon me, and branches of trees continuously bumped me."

Only the wave's motion back and forth across the valley saved him. "As I was swept on down toward the sea, half the time under water, the flood seemed to die away." He clambered to safety on a hill before the roar returned. He spent the next two nights making his way to safety at another farm.

But for every death-defying story, there were a dozen tragic ones. A team of naval men found six corpses in the Otay Valley, caught up in the few trees that had withstood the storm. A Japanese ranch hand reported that twenty members of his colony had died. A blacksmith named Silverthorn reported nineteen dead, apart from Gallagher and the Daneris. In the San Luis Rey River Valley, three women perished when the water surged as residents tried to rescue their furniture.

Although Otay bore the brunt of the casualties, it was becoming clear to Tulloch and everyone else at City Hall that the carnage was widespread across the county.

The rescue effort was launched from land, sea, and air.

Since dawn that morning, aviators had attempted to fly over the scene, with differing degrees of success. First into the air was the Cincinnati playboy and aviation enthusiast Colonel Max Fleischmann.

Arriving at Christmas for the "winter season," Fleischmann had installed his $12,000 mahogany flying boat on the North Island from where he'd announced his intention to "take spins daily in the lanes above the harbor." He had barely been up in the air since. After a fortnight of frustration, however, he finally got airborne that morning. But no sooner had he begun banking his plane inland than he was foundering in the still-gusting winds. The conditions were beyond him, and his plane nosedived to earth. By a minor miracle, he and his passenger walked away unscathed. His mahogany beauty was wrecked.

Later that afternoon, Howard Morin, a reporter from the *Union*, strapped himself into the passenger seat of a ninety-horsepower flying boat piloted by Raymond Morris of the Curtiss Aviation camp. For the next forty minutes, flying at 70 mph and a height of 200 feet and buffeted by winds and occasional cloudbursts, Morin was given the first bird's-eye view of the carnage.

The plane made straight for the Otay Valley. The dam's failure was immediately clear. Morin looked down on an "indescribable scene" filled with "wrecked and abandoned houses, devastated ranches and torn up fences and trees." The water unleashed by the dam's collapse was still "a veritable torrent, as its speed could be guessed by the trees and debris which floated on the surface." Matchstick-sized figures were visible, one group "employing a team of horses in pulling something from the swollen stream." A few miles inland from the bay, Morin and Morris saw three bodies, two men and a woman, lying facedown on a sand spit. Morris told Morin he thought the man "moved his hand as if to signal," but explained that it was impossible to land.

From the air the scale of the damage in the Tijuana Valley looked even greater. The racetrack had been inundated, with the track itself submerged and the pavilion tilted to one side. Lengthy sections of the San Diego & Arizona Railway and the San Diego & South Eastern Railway were washed out. Trains and carriages were strewn about like discarded toys. Bridges had simply disappeared. In the bay, Morin saw the steamship *Lucero* lying on her starboard side with debris piled all around. Another inlet, Glorietta Bay, was rimmed with dead horses.

Back on land at around 5:00 P.M., Morin reveled in the

momentary celebrity of becoming one of the first American reporters to use a plane to cover a disaster. "It was a wonderful trip," he wrote at his typewriter that evening. "But the scenes of desolation and destruction conveyed a feeling of depression that was hard to shake off."

Landowners and concerned relatives made their way by car.

Wallace Walter plowed his way through the mud back to the Otay Valley in his Hupmobile. Walter owned land all over the area and had been one of the last men to escape to the mountains before the landslides. "I went through Barrett Valley and down through Cottonwood. I never saw so much rain in my life, it came down like they had taken a bucket and just turned it over." He knew the rains had created carnage, but was stunned to see it firsthand. He described the scene at a railroad crossing. "It just took the railroad rails, parted them in the middle, and twisted them into horseshoes on each side of the rails."

A party including Sheriff Conklin headed to Otay via Palm City in a jitney. The vehicle slid and spun in the mud and had to be hauled at some points. Conklin knew many of Otay's residents. A two-story house belonging to City Justice Robinson, was "washed out to sea without even the signs of a foundation to mark where it once stood." The local Catholic church was gone. So were chicken farms, a pumping plant, and a gravel factory.

When they reached the point in the San Diego & Arizona Railway line where the new eighty-foot embankment should have been, they stood in an awed silence. Nothing remained. "The place was stripped as clean as a strip of desert land," said one member of the party. "It was as if a cannon ball had hit a pack of cards."

When a reporter from the *Union* found Elisha Babcock getting ready to leave his office on Fourth and Broadway, the businessman "had the appearance of a man who has lost sleep." Babcock was wearing galoshes, but his trousers were spattered with mud.

189

He called the loss of the Lower Otay Dam "a calamity." "I built just as good a dam as I could at that time. I did not believe that it would ever run over." He also admitted he had "contemplated putting an extra ten feet on it for the sake of additional safety."

Babcock knew there was talk of a grand-jury investigation and tried to focus on the future. He proposed that construction on a new dam should begin immediately "with the most substantial structure that can be erected." The "worried look" the reporter saw on Babcock's face was clearly echoed in his language. "No one regrets the occurrence more than I. It is a time when we should all pull together toward bigger things."

At least Babcock was not the sole subject of the city's anger. At his desk at City Hall, Seymour Tulloch was now hearing tales of heavy rains back in 1884. He came to believe that the Little Landers had been misled on the idea of farming river bottoms safely. "It is coming to light that there have been some floods in bygone years which have been conveniently forgotten while selling bottom lands to new comers at $1,000 an acre," he wrote.

"But of course no dams have gone out before. No such rainfall or rather 'runoff' has ever been known. It is something that no one has counted on seriously—and there have been years here without hardly a drop of rain—when everything burnt up. All of which goes to show the uncertainty of things and the dangers ever-lurking about water-courses even in 'dry' counties."

Mayor Edward Capps was forced to deny the latest rumor—of a water famine. "San Diegans need not be nervous a minute about a shortage of water," he said.

At the moment the city was drawing on the small reservoir at Chollas Heights. Capps said it was also possible to draw water from the Cuyamaca Dam, which could "furnish probably four or five million gallons a day." But the city was putting all its effort into fixing the Dulzura conduit—the link between Morena and the pipeline that ran down from the Lower Otay Dam. However,

Capps's reassurances proved a case of the right hand not knowing what the left was doing.

At around the same time the mayor was speaking, A. E. Banks, the city's health officer, confirmed the irony that was obvious to anyone who had turned on a faucet or dropped a pail down a well. "Owing to the turbidity of the San Diego drinking water," Banks warned, "it is earnestly recommended that the water used for drinking purposes be first boiled." He predicted a lengthy wait before the city's water would be back to normal. "Much animal and vegetable matter has been washed into the reservoirs and will be in suspension for some time."

NORMAL

[Federal Building, Saturday, January 29, 1916]

Cautiously, Herbert Nimmo and Dean Blake declared the worst over. With the wires down, the weathermen still couldn't get a weather forecast out. But they had watched the Federal Building barometer rising rapidly since 6:00 P.M. Thursday night. The 50 mph winds had gone, too. "Indications are that the storm of the last two days is over."

The skies over the city were flecked with a few high-level clouds, but on the horizon there were hints of coral, pearl, and azure, hues many had feared they would never see again. The weather was what Blake and Nimmo called "normal" for the time of year. But most San Diegans had lost all sense of what was normal anymore.

CLEAR

[Coronado, Sunday, January 30]

With her mother's health improving, Rose Dysart's weather note for the day might have summed up the atmosphere within the house on Coronado, too. "Clear," she wrote at the head of the page.

After days cooped up, Rose had left the house and headed to the bay with Helen that morning. It was invigorating to feel the sea breezes on her face again—even if they still carried strange and slightly disturbing odors with them. But it was still a shock when she saw the extent of the damage. She couldn't get over what the flood had done to the emerald waters of the harbor. "The Bay looks brown and muddy," she wrote in her diary later that day.

News of the disaster at Otay had spread quickly around the

tight-knit community out on Coronado. The Dysarts knew of the Daneris, but it was the loss of William Gallagher, who lived nearby with his young family, that seemed the cruelest. "It's just terrible," she had written in her diary the previous evening.

Rose didn't really know which of the death-toll figures to believe. Like everyone else she had read the newspaper reports, but she'd also heard people mutter of much higher numbers. What she saw with her own eyes that day inclined her to agree with the unpublished rumors. "Helen and I saw the torpedo boats looking for bodies in the bay. They say about sixty have been found," she recorded that evening.

PART V

The Conquering Hero
[January 31–May 1916]

Trail of Destruction. All that remained of the store in Otay, January 1916.
(San Diego Historical Society)

GAUGE

Morena, Monday, January 31, 1916
Height: 149.5 feet. Storage: 15 billion gallons

THE BENSON BROTHERS

[Jamul, Monday, January 31, 1916]

Charles and Paul picked their way through the pulverized land-scape warily, their rifles at the ready and their eyes alive to every movement around them.

With the phone line restored, Maggie Swenson had received an anonymous call that morning. "Tell that rainmaking idiot that we're on our way up to lynch him," the voice at the other end of the line warned.

Maggie defended Charles. "He's only done what he was asked to do."

"Well, his job's done and so is he," the man said before hanging up.

The Hatfield brothers had heard such talk before. In Los Angeles in 1905, a farmer had issued a warning to a newspaper, but its doggerel ("I'll buy me a shotgun—double barrel too, I'll load it with buckshot and aim it true") somehow softened the threat. This time Charles and Paul sensed they should take it seriously. The tower was left intact, and as always they buried their evaporation pans. They were heading down the mountain by midmorning.

The threat surprised Charles. At Morena the damage to the mountain landscape was minimal, and far outweighed by the bounty still flowing through the spillways at thousands of gallons an hour. He was expecting San Diego to laud him, not lynch him. The ravaged, rubble-strewn obstacle course he and Paul confronted as they descended into the valleys below Morena brought the reality home. "We didn't know anything about it," Paul remembered years later. "We could see it on our way down. Everything was gone. The road was gone, and bridges were gone."

The city continued to deal with its detritus and its dead.

At the quayside, the Brown Company's hoist had been given the job of salvaging telephone poles, wooden bridge girders and wine casks from the mountain of debris piled on the waterfront between Market Street and the municipal pier. The recoverable objects had to be separated from a morass of dead horses, live turtles, lizards, snakes, sections of railroad bridges, ties, pieces of household goods, and clothing.

Newspapers put out extra editions, with "known dead" displayed prominently. No one could agree on a precise number. The figure of sixty-five put out the previous day was now reckoned to be too high. The estimate of twenty that some were making seemed too low.

A total of eighteen fatalities were listed that morning. At the city's mortuaries however, many bodies remained unidentified: one was holding a "Japanese about 35 years old, smooth and shaven"; another had a "man about 45 years old, mustache and wearing shoes, believed to be a German." Two new Japanese bodies were found at Sweetwater. An unidentified male body was found buried near Murphy's Canyon in Mission Valley. Classified as "known dead not recovered" were "two Chinese" and "one Mexican" drowned in Mission Valley.

The undertakers faced additional problems. "You couldn't even get to the cemetery, the roads were impassable, plus the fact that you couldn't dig a grave," said one woman who had lost her father. She took her father's body to Roy Saum, a mortician at Johnson, Saum & Benbough, who organized a funeral at the Masonic Temple. Saum then took the body back to his parlor. "We couldn't bury him," complained the daughter. "They had to embalm him for two weeks."

The skies were clear but the air was soon heavy with a new threat: lawlessness.

Abandoned ranches and booty-strewn beaches became magnets for looters, some from across the border in Mexico. On the shore of San Diego Bay, police put cordons around the miniature mountains of furniture and farm equipment that spread out for miles. Anyone caught rummaging through the wreckage faced arrest.

A corps of forty U.S. Marines under Ensign Hamilton O'Brien of the cruiser *Milwaukee* patrolled the Otay Valley, from their garrison at the old school. O'Brien and his men were under orders to shoot on sight.

The weather remained the most feared force of all, however, and the city's edginess meant the flimsiest of rumors could spark panic. On Saturday evening, word spread of a 90 mph wind sweeping down the coast toward the city. It would hit San Diego at 10:00 P.M. With the weather bureau's credibility at a low ebb, Chief of Police Wilson didn't bother to check the story and simply raised the alarm. In the suburb of Ocean Beach, he phoned two homeowners, Charles Brummett and Herrick Cole, and asked them to alert their neighbors. Brummett and Cole careered through the streets barking through megaphones and soon persuaded half the neighborhood to evacuate. When another member of the police department called Blake and Nimmo at the weather bureau, he was assured that no warning had been received. The people of Ocean Beach crept home warily.

That same evening, another rumor whipped its way through the city's dockyards: the SS *Yale*, which had left San Diego for San Pedro earlier in the day, had sailed into the eye of the approaching storm and sunk. H. T. Krull, a representative of the ship's operators, quickly put out a denial—but it was too late to stop the story from racing through the rest of the city. Krull spent all night fielding calls from distraught friends and relatives.

As the day wore on, Paul's caution turned into paranoia. On the way down the mountain, they saw two men picking their way up along the narrow trail far below them. They broke away from the path to avoid them. The figures turned out to be George Cromwell and Rudolph Wueste from the water department, who were on their way up to Morena. When his bosses arrived at the dam later that day, Seth Swenson couldn't understand how the four men hadn't met.

The brothers' reception at Leon Smith's makeshift ferry across the Cottonwood only stoked Paul's unease. Smith owned an olive grove and a busy camp station where teams of horses and herds of cattle stopped for water and feed on their way down to San Diego. He was now charging people fifty cents to haul them across the river in a tea chest he had fixed to a pulley and a rope.

The two scruffy strangers were the first people who had made it down from Morena in days.

"Did you see Hatfield up there?" the ferryman asked Paul.

"Yes," Paul replied, his protective instincts at work. "He was up there."

Like everyone else in the city, Smith had doubtless read the descriptions of the rainmaking brothers. The sight of two waist-coated strangers aroused his suspicion. But when he asked their name, Paul replied "Benson."

"That was the best thing to do," Paul remembered later. "To take no chances."

The light was fading and the brothers inquired about bed and board. Smith offered the nearest of his two homes. Charles and Paul spent the night in the shadow of Morena. But it was the animus awaiting them in San Diego that darkened their dreams.

HIDING

[San Diego, February 3, 1916]

B y the time he reached the outskirts of the city, Hatfield had been on his feet for four days. He was exhausted and close to collapse.

On his way down, he had heard explosions in the hills behind him. Someone told him that along the ruined mountain roads, the cleanup operation was being carried out by huge metal road scrapers hauled by four-horse teams and two-man teams of dynamiters.

The air still carried the salty tang of the sea but was now flavored with the charcoal smoke of bonfires and the faint aroma of decaying livestock. At the Sweetwater River, where the main gas pipeline had been fractured, it was sickly-sweet.

Passing through the communities at the southern edge of the

city, Hatfield found himself stopping and staring at the mangled remains of railway lines, bloated animal carcasses, discarded and submerged vehicles. In the distance, on the bay itself, it looked as if vast mountains of seaweed had piled up. As he got closer, he realized it was the rubble of broken homes.

Although the *Union* printed a photo of Hatfield during the first storm, no one could have matched that clean-cut portrait with the latest bedraggled, mud-caked figure to limp into the city from the backcountry. Most of the stories now circulating placed him far from San Diego. According to one of the rumors, he had fled Morena, the mountains, and the state itself and was en route to Yuma, Arizona, on horseback. If another was to be believed, he had slipped across the border into Mexico.

The San Diego papers were eager to get hold of the miracle man of Morena and had spent the past days watching the rain-maker's in-laws. Jennie Rulon remained one of Hatfield's most defiant defenders. On Monday she told the *Union* her son-in-law was misunderstood. "From the fact that for four years he has been employed in the San Joaquin Valley to make it rain, and has collected his money and satisfied the people there, there is possibly more merit in his undertaking than many will believe. If the Morena has overflown we may expect him here shortly. If it has not he will remain there until it does."

The first person Hatfield made contact with was Fred Binney, who arranged for a room in a "safe" house. He led Charles and Paul there around dusk. The brothers immediately collapsed on their beds, overwhelmed by exhaustion.

Since the rain started, Binney hadn't missed an opportunity to press Charles's case with the city council. In a typically florid letter to the *Union*, he used comparative statistics to argue that a genuine miracle was occurring at Morena. Binney pointed out that the Cuyamaca Dam collected an average of 36 inches of rain per year compared to Morena's 21.5 inches. Yet through January

27, Cuyamaca was 4.79 inches short of its average and Morena was 4.5 inches ahead of its average. "Here we have scientific proof," Binney wrote. The *Union* printed it dutifully, underneath a banner headline that read what HATFIELD HAS DONE. Naturally it also carried the usual caveat: "As F. A. Binney Sees It."

At his office, he was now working on Charles's official report to Cosgrove and the city. He shared this information with a reporter from the *Union* that evening. "I haven't been able to sell much real estate lately, so I thought I'd go into the water business," he added. He also confirmed the return to the city of the most wanted man in San Diego. Binney did so with a word of warning: "Anyone who has in mind shooting the rainmaker would better be quick as Hatfield has been practicing whipping a gun from his hip pocket."

NOT DEAD

[8th and C Streets, Friday, February 4, 1916]

My name is Ober, William Ober," announced the latest emaciated figure to limp into the lobby of the *Union* offices on 2nd Street. Ober claimed he had spent days in a tree after his ranch house was carried down the Tijuana. "I am not dead. I am very much alive. Just put that in your paper, will you?" He might have been speaking for the entire city.

The flood had put San Diego on every newswire from Los Angeles to London, Brisbane to Bombay. Thousands of miles away from the scene of the disaster, headline writers imagined California, home of unimaginable earthquakes and droughts, had once more witnessed an event of biblical magnitude.

The Associated Press's syndicated bulletin talked of "65 dead," "all communications cut off," and "charming little valleys desolate." In Helena, Montana, a newspaper headline had SAN DIEGO WIPED OFF MAP. In Iowa, the city had been "Washed Into Sea." Countless papers had written of the "San Diego Disaster." The *Oakland Tribune* had "3,000 Are Homeless."

As wires reconnected the city to the nation, the city's boosters became alarmed by the fallout. Attendance at the Exposition was already suffering. The threat to its prospects for the rest of the year was clear. The search for a scapegoat began with the usual shooting of the messenger.

The two main newspapers, the *Union* and the *Sun*, blamed each other for the outside world's misguided views. As tempers calmed, Aubrey Davidson persuaded the council to make February 11 "Exposition Letter Writing Day." The city's schools agreed to dedicate an hour of their students' time to the plan. Every child in the city would write to a friend or relative outside the city to tell them San Diego hadn't disappeared into the ocean.

Slowly the city began putting a positive spin on things. The Exposition led the way. Its best booster, D. C. Collier, set off on a tour of California to drum up support, and an exhibit of twelve-foot animal cages was being constructed in a rush. A collection of lions, pumas, leopards, monkeys, bears, and a solitary kangaroo were acquired, along with a professional trainer. The animals would star in a free twice-daily show. Anything to get in the crowds again.

The mood was soon picked up in the papers. Articles played down the deaths and celebrated the city's good fortune in acquiring so much rainwater. "In truth the benefits of the recent heavy rains offset the damage done in the back country. This opinion is voiced by practically all persons who have been on a trip through the county in the past few days," ran a typical *Union* piece that railed against "exaggerated and distorted reports of flood damage published by out-of-town papers."

"This country is not going to the bow wows, in spite of what a few pessimists may think," said a spokesman for a local bank.

City officials made a virtue of the fact that the Santa Fe Railroad was taking on 1,500 men to rebuild the line, that the Hercules Powder Company was hiring 200 workers to rebuild its plant in National City, and that the county supervisors were using hundreds of laborers to rebuild roads and bridges. "It's an ill wind that blows no one any good," the *Los Angeles Times* reported, "and the ill wind that blew floods and damage into San Diego county also blew thousands of idle men work at good wages repairing the damage caused by the recent rains."

No amount of positive thinking could change the ruinous reality many faced, however. On Sheridan Avenue, a man named Kinaird had just seen his eight acres of oranges ripen for the first time when the floods wiped them out. With the railroad still out and no prospect of recovering his business, he grew tired of the sight of his wasted land. "He became so discouraged and so despondent about not being able to harvest his nice little crop of oranges that he crawled up in the loft of his hay barn, put a rope around his neck, dropped off in a few bales of hay and hanged himself," said his neighbor Paul Hatch. "He lost interest in life."

"Shaved and shined up," Hatfield smiled broadly for the photographers outside the press conference Fred Binney had called at his office. Alongside him Binney, dressed like Charles in a well-pressed three-piece suit, brimmed with something akin to paternal pride. Charles exuded quiet triumph. "His entire demeanor was that of the proverbial conquering hero home from the front and awaiting the laurel wreath," wrote one witness the next day.

As the conference got under way, it was clear the reporters were not quite ready to garland him. Hatfield couldn't contain his excitement at what he believed he had achieved. "He smiled continually and talked so rapidly that it was difficult to cut in with a question," wrote one reporter.

He was in no mood to undersell himself. "I might keep on with my tests until domesday and could not show the Council more convincing proof of my work than I already have done," he said, adding that he considered himself "responsible for fully fifteen inches of the rain that fell up there." He recalled all the warnings about rain-laden clouds that sailed overhead without dispensing rain. "None of them got away while I was there, I can tell you!"

However, he was not so giddy that he was going to give away his secrets. "If I told you everything, rainmakers would spring up like mushrooms." Nor was he going to answer questions about how much he had spent. "I spent my own money and would have stayed out there until December if it had been necessary to remain there that long to fulfill my end of the contract. Who would have been the sufferer then?"

He did confirm that he had used more chemicals than ever before. "My test at Morena was the most potent I ever have made," he said. "I used 100 percent stronger forces than ever before."

He was not surprised when someone asked him to account for the fact that it had rained hard all over the state. "I expected that question," he said. "But you will remember that it often rains as hard around Los Angeles as it did this year but that San Diego gets only a small part of the rainfall in this end of the state."

Charles's answer to the suggestion that if he collected the $10,000 he should also meet any liability for damage reflected the boosterish positivism he had picked up in the papers. "My answer to that is that for every dollar which has been suffered in damages there will be a thousand dollars in benefits. Fixing up the roads and the bridges and the like will give employment to thousands of idle men, will put lots of money in circulation and help business tremendously. . . . I have had a number of merchants tell me that already they have felt the increase in business."

Charles's smile cracked only when someone brought up the deaths and asked, "Do you think that a life can be measured in financial terms?"

After a pause, he grimaced and replied, "That is terrible, and no one is more sorry than I am, but I do not feel that I am in any way responsible for that."

Throughout the press conference, Fred Binney tried—and failed—to impose himself on the proceedings. When he finally managed to interrupt Charles, it was to declare the conference over. He told the reporters they were headed for an important meeting—with Terence Cosgrove.

IMPLIED

[City Hall, Wednesday, February 9, 1916]

F ive days later, Hatfield emerged onto the steps of City Hall, ran his fingers through his hair, and fixed his fedora in place. Greeting passersby as he stepped out on to the street, his smile was broad, but, he hoped, not too reminiscent of the cat that had gotten into the cream.

He had arrived midmorning to present his twelve-page report to Terence Cosgrove and was, at first, disappointed. He was told that the city attorney had been urgently called to Los Angeles and wasn't expected back until the end of the week.

Charles asked to read his report to the city council and was refused even that. They agreed to refer it to Cosgrove as soon as he returned.

It was a conversation with a reporter from the *San Diego Sun*

HATFIELD DRAWS UP HIS BILL FOR THE COUNCIL

Rainmaker Is Now Preparing Official Demand for $10,000; Declares in Document That Council Should Carry Out Agreement and Pay Him for Filling Morena Dam; City Solons Must Make Decision Soon.

An Official Demand. A report on Hatfield's claim. *San Diego Sun*, Wednesday, February 9, 1916.

that improved his mood. The reporter collared Hatfield as he was heading out of the council chamber. Given the amount of work he'd put into his report, Charles was excited to put its contents into the public domain. The reporter was soon scribbling away in his notepad.

Charles divided his report into three sections: the first dealt with his understanding of the "implied contract" between him and San Diego, the second with the rainfall and runoff figures for the month he had spent at Morena, and the final part with his previous successes.

It was obvious what the city's argument would be: A widespread storm had hit the whole state. So Charles began with a reiteration of his basic philosophy: "You will remember that I distinctly told you when I addressed you that I did not claim to produce rain from a cloudless sky, but to increase precipitation to convert a one-inch rainfall into a three-inch rainfall (so to speak)."

He went on to emphasize Morena's notoriously changeable conditions. "I was informed on my arrival at Morena that favorable indications for rain were frequently present, but that they would vanish and dissipate without letting their moisture

211

descend. While I had my demonstrations in force at Morena each and every time that conditions were present, rain fell in torrents."

Fred Binney's influence was clearly at work. Hatfield claimed that the rainfall at Cuyamaca between January 27 and 30 was also "due to my operations as the two watersheds are within a few miles of each other." He missed no opportunity to remind the city how valuable a windfall they now had sitting in the mountains. "The cash value of the 4,000,000 gallons of water that is the least that can be attributed to me at Morena is $400,000 at 10 cents a 1,000," he said. "You agreed to pay me $10,000 and I maintain that your city council never made a better bargain for the taxpayers."

All in all, he concluded, the filling of Morena was "surely a wonderful undertaking." And while there was no formal contract, the council had an "honorable liability" to pay him in full.

Hatfield happily answered the *Sun* reporter's questions about the document. He had read the accounts of his performance at Fred Binney's press conference, so today he tried to strike a more measured and modest note. "Will you tell the people that I do not consider my $10,000 charge the biggest feature of my work here. It is just incident to the work. My real interest is in the good that can be accomplished in this comparatively arid country by scientific rain producing. It is not a one-man question, but is a matter of great importance to all the people of San Diego County."

But what really lifted Hatfield's spirits was the way the conversation turned after he ran through his report. The reporter told Charles he had heard strong rumors that Cosgrove was going to accept his claim. Until now Charles had not allowed himself to get too optimistic, but this did validate his own impression. In his meeting with Charles after the press conference days earlier, the attorney seemed friendly and simply reiterated what he had told Binney before. Charles had only to provide a detailed summary of the operations at Morena. Then they could move on to the contract he had drawn up.

The reporter told Charles that, in the wake of that meeting and others within City Hall, Cosgrove had all but accepted Charles's case. "Cosgrove has expressed an opinion that there was a 'contract implied,' " the reporter said. "The city is bound in honor to pay for the fulfillment of the contract."

Hatfield left City Hall convinced the $10,000 was in the bag. He headed west into the city to catch a tram back up to Kansas Avenue, bursting to share the news.

Heading down Broadway, he passed the Plaza Cinema. It was showing a local film, made by Lubin's Coronado Company and billed as "A Masterful Drama With Sounds Made In San Diego." He would have done well to dwell on the film's title; it was called *The Law's Injustice*.

LOWS

[Federal Building, Saturday, February 12, 1916]

To judge by its official report, the U.S. Weather Bureau wasn't entirely sure what had hit San Diego. In the next edition of *Monthly Weather Review*, the meteorologists in Washington guessed the storms were caused by two "lows" that had passed over California. But their convoluted account—which ultimately blamed the flooding on saturated soil—was anything but convincing.

Dean Blake, however, was certain of what had *not* caused the storm. Publicly, at the Federal Building, he and Herbert Nimmo maintained a dismissive silence about Charles's pronouncements. But in private Blake told anyone who wanted to hear his opinion. "It certainly sounds very foolish of him to have asserted that the gases which he caused to rise produced abnormally heavy precipitation from the Mexican to the Canadian border."

WHAT NATURE DID

[City Hall, Thursday, February 17, 1916]

As Hatfield made his way to the mayor's chamber, he breathed in San Diego's rediscovered optimism. The sun was beating down and the feeling that the city was getting back on its feet was palpable.

That morning the Santa Fe Railway Company announced that the track rebuilding was finished ahead of schedule. The thousands of men employed to relay the tracks around Oceanside had outdone themselves. The first train from Los Angeles since January 18 was due in San Diego at 12:50 Friday afternoon—exactly one month after service was suspended.

From Hatfield's point of view, even better news that morning came from Morena. George Cromwell had come down from the mountains and pronounced himself satisfied that the dam was

215

now safe; he also revealed the final impoundment figures. According to Seth Swenson's gauge, the dam contained 13.461 billion gallons of water. More than 2.5 billion gallons had been released into the system below since January 27.

Charles knew his way around City Hall by now and made for the mayor's chamber. The small gathering of city officials, councilmen, and reporters waiting for him saw the same calm, professional confidence he had displayed back in December. Only a few of them knew how misplaced it was.

As in December, Mayor Capps took charge of the proceedings. He opened the meeting by asking, "What do you desire this conference to do, Mr. Hatfield?"

Charles stood and looked the mayor straight in the eye. "The essence of my contract was to fill Morena reservoir; this has been done." He emphasized the final four words in a way that left no one in any doubt of the pride he felt in delivering them. "I have fulfilled my contract and desire that the city should fulfill its contract to pay me $10,000."

Capps didn't reply; instead, he deferred to Terence Cosgrove.

"How much water do you claim to have put in Morena?" Cosgrove asked.

In his written submission to the council, Hatfield had erred on the side of caution and humility. He knew the figures inside out. But he felt it wrong to claim the full amount.

"Four billion gallons, if not more," he replied.

Cosgrove could have indulged himself in a theatrical look of puzzlement but didn't. "But you agreed to put in ten billions," he responded.

Charles was eager to explain. "There were five billion gallons in the reservoir when I started work, and it required fifteen billions to fill the reservoir. I claim that through the instrumentality of my work four billion gallons was put into the reservoir and the other was the indirect result of my work."

For Cosgrove it now became an exercise involving fish, a

shotgun, and a barrel. "You want the city to pay you only for what you yourself did," he said sharply. "You do not want the city to pay you for what Nature did, do you?"

Charles kept his composure and simply said, "No."

"Well," Cosgrove responded, "why do you ask the city to pay you for ten billion gallons when you put in only four billion gallons?"

In the past, Charles overcame skepticism by drawing on his evangelical self-belief, his widespread reputation for honesty, and a gift for being verbose and factually vague at the same time. "He could talk more and say less than any man I met," recalled a town official who encountered him in Hemet, California. If all else failed he delivered one of his peculiar smiles and introduced another "draught in the conversation."

Cosgrove was not about to allow him to get away with either.

Hatfield's composure suddenly deserted him. For a moment he looked lost. Before he could regain his thread, Cosgrove turned away and theatrically began addressing the councilmen.

"According to his own statement," he said, "this man has admitted that he put only four billion gallon of water in the reservoir. He offered to deliver ten billion gallons. Therefore he has not fulfilled his contract, and there is no liability on the part of the city. He should have waited until he has fulfilled his contract."

The grisly spectacle had been underway for only a few minutes but it was already turning one of the councilmen's stomachs. Walter Moore rose and told the meeting his understanding of the contract: Hatfield should receive his money if Morena overflowed, regardless of what the cause might be. "I think he should be paid his money," he added.

Now Cosgrove's voice acquired even more steel. He looked directly at Moore and went on the attack:

If I give a ruling on this matter, it will be based solely upon the facts as shown by the records, and not upon any understandings or upon anybody's sympathy. The records show that Hatfield made three propositions to the city.

The resolution which was passed by the Council simply said that Hatfield's offer was accepted, but it did not say which of the three propositions was accepted.

This is the situation which confronts anyone who has the responsibility of deciding whether or not Hatfield has a legal claim against the city. The courts are not going to be guided by my understanding or anyone else's understanding but solely by the facts. The facts show there on the record for themselves. I cannot say that he has or has not increased the rainfall at Morena, and what I or anyone else thinks about it is of no consequence.

A sense of shock settled on the chamber. Cosgrove had the floor to himself and continued by returning to Charles's visibly crumbling figure.

"This gentleman, according to my opinion, cannot collect his money in the courts. Under the constitution and the statutes of the state and the charter of the city, a claim that is unenforceable is invalid."

Charles's main opponents on the council, Fox and Fay, moved in. Fox proposed, and Fay seconded, a motion that the matter be left to Cosgrove. Cosgrove said he would provide a full written opinion on the matter.

Percy Benbough joined Moore in voting against the motion. He didn't disagree with Cosgrove's legal analysis. Like Moore, he simply thought San Diego was morally bound to pay Charles.

"Four councilmen voted to accept this man's proposition and told him to go ahead," said Benbough. "He ought to be paid."

Moments later, the meeting was adjourned. Charles rushed out of the chamber ashen-faced, his head bowed.

UNFAIR

[Kansas Avenue, Friday, February 18, 1916]

A t his in-laws' home on Kansas Avenue, Charles paced the living room endlessly, repeating the same questions in his mind.

Hadn't he done what he was contracted to do, and even factored in—out of fairness—a recognition of the wider weather conditions? Hadn't Cosgrove been leaning his way just a week earlier? What had changed his mind? And why hadn't he fought back in the meeting? Small aftershocks of emotion were now emerging: anger, frustration, and embarrassment. The sickening knot in his stomach tightened each time he looked at the headline in the morning edition of the *Union*: HATFIELD IS REFUSED PAYMENT BY COUNCIL.

Charles turned to the court of public opinion. He put out a statement, railing at the unfairness of Cosgrove's decision. "It was never even hinted that I was to be paid only my pro rata of the 10,000,000 gallons and the city was to be credited with what nature put in. This is an unfair construction of my contract, and in my filed report I remind the council that I told them I did not claim to produce rain from a cloudless sky, but to convert a light rainfall into a heavy one, which of course implies that when I am at work nature is at work also."

At the same time, with Binney's help, he organized interviews with anyone willing to hear his side. Hatfield sincerely believed that he had played his part in filling Morena. The money was important, but getting the credit was just as vital.

Like the city itself, journalists were confused about what to think.

Alfred Robinson of the Exposition's *California Garden* magazine was charmed by Charles's straightforward smile. "He has not the appearance of a bloated monopolist though I believe his particular field is very much his own, nor does he carry any of that air of pity for ordinary mortals that is the special garment of those who know more than the rest of us in their own estimations."

"I do not stand sponsor for Hatfield but he seems full of confidence in himself and his perseverance against the jeers of the multitude entitle him to respect." But when it came to the question of whether Charles was responsible for the storms, Robinson pleaded bafflement: "I don't know."

Charles's supporters didn't give up. Walter Moore bowled into City Hall waving a motion he intended to introduce at the council's Monday meeting, at which Cosgrove would make his decision formal. Moore's motion proposed that the city hire Charles for five years, at a salary of $12,000 a year. He thought this was the least the council do, considering that the rainmaker had been instrumental in "furnishing this city with the cheapest and best water of any on the coast." Hatfield's permanent role would more than reimburse him for the loss of the $10,000 that he expected would be paid him if the Morena was filled.

"I am not one bit superstitious," Moore stated in his motion, "neither do I wish to be thought sacrilegious in saying that, in my opinion, Mr. Hatfield can assist the Almighty in his endeavors to beautify this, His beauty spot of America."

However, Terence Cosgrove's attitude toward the situation was hardening. He knew the first lawsuits were imminent and that to defend them successfully the city would need the storms defined as "acts of God." Everything in his training told him the city could not implicate itself as being responsible in any way. He even vetoed a decision by the city council to award Seth Swenson a medal for his bravery in saving Morena.

The truth about Swenson's actions in the early hours of January 28 had emerged when Wueste and Cromwell made it up to Morena. The council had been unanimous in approving their recommendation of an honor. But as Walter Bellon of the health department later put it, "the whole beautiful dream blew up. . . . The city attorney stepped in and blocked the resolution of valor, by stating that the dam keeper was hired, housed and paid to perform such duties as may become necessary for the dam's safety and that such measures were successfully carried out, is no such reason to glorify the simple basic duties or the man that carried them thru."

COUNTING THE COST

[San Diego, Sunday, February 20, 1916]

T wo members of the U.S. Geological Survey, F. C. Ebert and H. D. McGlashan, arrived in San Diego and began the most extensive survey of the flood damage.

Ebert had been given an inkling of the damage in January. He set off for San Diego from Los Angeles on January 17, but made it no farther than Oceanside. He had to wait almost three weeks before his car could be hauled across the river.

The inventory they began assembling that week would eventually be presented in a report. Their document would read like a set of annual accounts, filled with cold tabulations and hard statistics. The human cost of the storms would lie in the details.

In the farming communities of the river valleys they found "large areas whose agricultural value was almost completely destroyed. . . . An example is afforded by a tract of land in Otay Valley formerly used as a truck garden and valued at $1,000 per acre; after the flood 11 acres of this land were sold at a foreclosure sale for $100."

Their report split damages into five categories: agricultural land, municipal buildings, water supply, highways and bridges, and "miscellaneous." The latter category included the destruction of twenty-three of the geological survey's own recording stations. But their loss was nothing compared to the Fenton-Sumption-Barnes gravel-washing plant, where $35,000 worth of buildings and equipment had been wiped off the map. "This plant was a complete loss, for after the flood there was not an indication on the surface to show its location."

The damage at the Western Salt Company was even costlier. Its supply of 2,500 tons of salt had been lost, as had all its brine ponds. In all, 170 acres of salt ground had been buried under a deep deposit of silt. The total damage was $85,500. There was a rich, unspoken irony in the plant's devastation: The company's main shareholder was Elisha S. Babcock, and the breach of the dam he designed effectively finished him as a force in San Diego business.

"LICKED"

[Point Loma, Saturday, February 26, 1916]

harles and Paul blended into the sardine-tin crush at the municipal pier and squeezed their way onto the morning steamer bound for San Pedro and Los Angeles. During the past four days their sense of anger and shock had atrophied into bitterness.

On Monday, with Walter Moore's help, Charles had persuaded the council to hear him one more time. He wanted to be reasonable, but he didn't want anyone to think he was not serious about his threat of legal action.

He stuck to his figure of 4 billion gallons and suggested a price of $1,000 per billion gallons. It was no longer a matter of money, he told the council. He claimed he had spent the extraordinary sum of $3,000 at Morena.

"If this council does not sanction my offer," he said, "I shall be compelled against my inclinations to bring suit against the city."

After a brief debate, it was agreed to refer the matter to Terence Cosgrove once more. Cosgrove knew his answer immediately, but dragged the matter out until Friday. "My opinion is that the Hatfield claim in unenforceable and consequently invalid," he wrote in his opinion, presented to the council and made public that day. "If the council is of my opinion, I recommend that the claim and offer of compromise be rejected. If you are of the opinion that the claim is valid and enforceable, I recommend that you accept the offer." No one dared challenge him.

As a last resort, Charles visited several attorneys in the city.

"He wanted to know if he could collect: but nothing doing," said Paul. "We saw at once that we were licked." News of their defeat at the hands of Cosgrove filled the papers. HATFIELD AGAIN GIVEN THE HOOK, ran the headline in the *Sun*.

"Charles was very indignant," Paul said later. Like his brother, he was certain their tower had played its part in extracting the extra moisture at Morena. "We designed the whole works and they got a million dollars' worth of water for nothing."

Yet, like Charles, he recognized that—for now—it was time to retreat.

The steamer eased its way off the quayside and glided across the emerald waters of the bay to Point Loma. From there it headed north past the mouth of Mission Bay. As the ship's engines settled into their rhythm, the pockets of passengers on the deck watched San Diego receding into the distance. In the morning light, they could make out the matchstick figures of people pacing the beaches. The beachcombers were still scouring the shoreline for the latest treasures to be washed down from the hills above them.

THE PIED PIPER

[Balboa Park, May 27, 1916]

O n the morning of Saturday, May 27, a vast crowd began gathering at the edge of the Exposition's grounds in Balboa Park. The day's big event, a full-scale reenactment of *The Pied Piper of Hamelin*, had been trumpeted by the newspapers for days and succeeded in attracting most of the city's children. Starched and pressed in their Sunday best, an estimated thirteen thousand of them gathered by the western entrance to the park, at Cabrillo Bridge, around 11:00 A.M. Their excited chattering could be heard several blocks away.

The event was easily the most ambitious entertainment staged since the storm.

San Diego's thirty-two-day disconnection from the rest of the world hit the Exposition hard, forcing Aubrey Davidson to move back his original reopening date in mid-February. The formal rededication had gone ahead, as planned in March, but attendance figures were so poor that in April, Davidson got the newspapers to question the city's loyalty with a *Union* editorial imploring: "Support the Exposition." The faint air of panic hadn't been eased by the success of the area's other tourist attractions, the bars, bordellos, and gambling joints opening almost weekly across the border in Tijuana. To counter this, the Exposition brought in roulette nights and a revue of scantily clad dancers, the Sultan's Harem but it only brought more woe. Days after it opened to bumper audiences, the county's district attorney closed the harem down for being too lewd.

At the end of a rocky period, the Pied Piper provided a perfect platform to publicly apportion the blame for the Exposition's sliding fortunes.

A city trustee named Hubert Collins soon appeared as the Piper. Dressed in the quartered yellow and red costume made famous in Maxfield Parrish's illustrations of the Browning poem, Collins began by chasing a hundred rat-costumed children into a small lake. He then returned to the main stage where five city burghers were waiting.

The make-believe politicians, led by City Solicitor Charles Jackson playing the mayor, milked their moment for all it was worth. Jackson dramatically announced that he now intended to pay the Piper just $10 rather than the $5,000 he had been promised.

> *So, friend, we're not the folks to shrink*
> *From the duty of giving you something to drink*
> *And a matter of money to put in your poke*
> *But, as for the dollars, what we spoke*
> *Of them, as you very well know, was in joke.*

As they warmed to the task, the actors broke off from Browning's text to improvise an exchange that alluded to the city's own version of the German allegory. "The Council and the piper engaged in

227

some witty dialogue in which San Diego's recent experience with rainmaker Hatfield was referred to," observed the *Los Angeles Times*'s reporter. The off-the-cuff banter was lost on most of the younger audience, but drew appreciative laughs from the adults.

The show ended with the Piper leading the hordes of children away, across the main entrance to the Exposition site, the Cabrillo Bridge. As the "bobbing hats and hair bows" filed into the Exposition grounds, the children looked every inch the personification of Browning's infant victims:

> *All the little boys and girls,*
> *With rosy cheeks and flaxen curls,*
> *And sparkling eyes and teeth like pearls,*
> *Tripping and skipping, ran merrily after*
> *The wonderful music with shouting and laughter.*

The show had one last theatrical flourish. As the parents watched their children disappear into the Pied Piper's cavern (a man-made mountain at the elaborate Panama Canal concession building) the air was suddenly filled with the sound of "dreadful thunder and lightning." The noise was being made by a team of special-effects artists inside the building, but was so convincing it caught the adults on the other side of the Cabrillo Bridge off guard. Reflexively, many found themselves looking upward to the heavens.

Not so long ago, San Diego's skies had been something to brag about. Now they were something to be feared.

PART VI

The Man the Rain Minds [1916–1958]

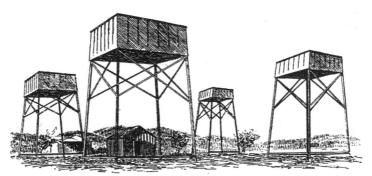

Plant for Precipitating Rain

"The Tower of Showers." An artist's impression of Hatfield's rainmaking towers in Crow's Landing, 1907–08. (Uncredited clipping in Hatfield Papers, San Diego Public Library)

ACT OF GOD

On Saturday, December 2, 1916, a lawyer from Los Angeles, representing Hatfield, walked into the San Diego city attorney's office and sat down for a meeting with Terence Cosgrove and his deputy, Shelley Higgins.

The lawyer had just served a summons on Mayor Capps. Attached was a suit—*Charles M. Hatfield, Plaintiff v. The City of San Diego, a Municipal Corporation, Defendant*—claiming full payment of $10,000 for filling the Morena Reservoir. Cosgrove had dismissively added the suit to the long list of those filed since January. But when Hatfield's lawyer suggested a private talk, he couldn't help letting his curiosity get the better of him.

"We got the impression the rainmaker still was eager for compromise," Higgins wrote later. But compromise wasn't a concept

Cosgrove had much interest in. The exchanges were short and sweet.

Higgins remembered: "We told the attorney that if Hatfield would sign a statement assuming all responsibility for the flood and absolve the City, we would recommend to the Council that every nickel of his claim be paid. Hatfield's attorney told us to 'Go to hell.' "

From Hatfield's perspective, signing the sort of statement Cosgrove proposed would be financial suicide. He knew how hard the floods had hit the city's purse.

With a blend of bribery and shrewdness, Cosgrove had been able to settle some of the compensation claims. A claim by Elisha Babcock was rejected because Cosgrove said it was filed too late. Only two major claims were heading for court, one of which was by Manuel Daneri. But the cost of rebuilding the city remained daunting. The report by the geological survey put the total bill at almost $3.7 million. The damage to agricultural land was $1.5 million; to municipal buildings, $72,850; to the water supply, $1,225,000; to highways and bridges, $652,350; and to "miscellaneous," $231,427.

Hatfield could not afford to lose $10,000, let alone figures of that magnitude. At this same time, however, he could less afford to lose his reputation. At some point he came to the decision that he should try to strike a deal of some kind with Cosgrove.

In a note attached to the city's book of records, there is a reference to a letter written sometime between February and December in which Hatfield offered to repudiate his claims for $10,000 and then $4,000 "for the city's benefit." The note explains: "He wanted to do this so no one could say that he failed as a rainmaker."

When Hatfield's lawyer sat down with Terence Cosgrove, he probably had a deal in mind whereby the city would somehow acknowledge Charles's part in the event. The reception he received from Cosgrove explains why it was never raised again.

Terence Cosgrove's determination to brush the whole episode

under the carpet was also understandable. In public-relations terms, the flood had caused the city real damage.

San Diego's Exposition was winding down as planned, and was ready to close at the end of December. Attendance figures had rallied and by the end of the year well over one million people had visited Balboa Park. A feeling persisted long afterward, however, that the negative publicity brought by the floods—and Hatfield's association with them—had somehow taken the shine off the event.

Unlike the Exposition, Charles's case against San Diego dragged into 1917 and beyond. His chances rested on a judge's deciding that the floods had been caused by forces other than nature. The two other flood-related cases that made it to court were both heard outside San Diego—one in Orange County and the other in San Bernardino County—and both lowered Charles's hopes. On both occasions, the courts found in favor of the city council by deciding the storms had been "acts of God."

The decision devastated Manuel Daneri and ruined his hopes of rebuilding his winery. His daughter-in-law remembered, "They said it was an act of God, and nobody got anything. Everybody in the valley lost. But if they had kept that dam in good condition, it wouldn't have gone out. The Daneris lost everything, all their wine, their ranch, everything they had."

Hatfield kept his suit on the books and was encouraged by the departure of Terence Cosgrove, who resigned his post in order to start his own firm, Hunsaker, Britt and Cosgrove. The ongoing lawsuit occasionally brought him back to the city. His visits offered him glimpses of a San Diego entering a new phase in its history, one shaped by the tumultuous events of 1916.

In a sense, like the Pied Piper, Charles played his part in relieving the city of its youthful innocence.

The devastation in San Ysidro effectively ended the eight-year dream of the Little Landers. By the end of World War I, everyone had left. In the mountains above the city, too, the floods ended a pioneering era. "Much was gone forever," wrote Dorothy

Clark Schmid of the aftermath of the flood. "Never again was there to be such individual independence." For all its troubles, the Exposition, too, played a big role in setting San Diego on its way as a mature city. The opening of the Panama Canal predictably increased its maritime profile, and the U.S. Navy became its dominant industrial force. San Diego became famous for its aviation, too, home to two of its great pioneers; Glenn Curtiss and Charles Lindbergh. But the industrialization was not to the liking of those who'd shared Aubrey Davidson's vision of "a paradise of the Western hemisphere."

The argument over its future crystallized in the 1917 mayoral race, a contest that became universally known as Smokestacks versus Chrysanthemums. It was an argument the city never quite resolved.

After years of inactivity, Hatfield's case was finally dismissed as a "dead issue" on May 28, 1938. Legally, at least, the decision brought the argument over who caused the San Diego floods to an end.

But the real debate over Charles's role in the extraordinary events of January 1916 would never end. Especially while he continued practicing his strange craft with such seeming success.

RAIN ENOUGH

J ust as Hatfield had hoped, Morena reignited his career and lifted his profile to new heights. Controversy dogged him, of course, but the next decade and a half provided him with moments to rank among the highlights of his career.

In the immediate aftermath of the Morena "contract," drought-afflicted farmers remained his staple clients. In 1917, a millionaire named Jameson, from the town of Taft, California, paid well above the going rate—$1,500 an inch—for a successful contract with Charles. In February 1918, Charles was hired by farmers in Chino, south of Pomona, at his normal rate of $1,000 an inch.

When America entered the war in Europe, Charles had to make do without Paul, who was drafted into the army as a private. He served briefly in France and returned unscathed.

In August 1919, Charles's notoriety soared when *Everybody's*, one of America's best-selling magazines, ran an interview with "The Man the Rain Minds." Beneath a photograph of Hatfield studiously dispensing chemicals in a laboratory, the article treated Charles with an unquestioning reverence that came close to sycophancy. In return, he gave away more than usual. "There is no magic in my method," he said. "It is only scientific." He went on to explain how he evaporated chemicals to produce "cirrus clouds, the fore-runners of rain clouds . . . In a short time these cirrus clouds develop into a nimbus, or rain cloud."

Hatfield couldn't resist inflating the number of successes he had racked up. "You can understand that luck isn't going to favor the same man something like five hundred times and running," he said.

To the millions who read the piece, the exaggeration mattered little. In a dark year for America, marred by strikes, racial tension, and a worsening economic climate, Hatfield was just the sort of arresting, unusual, and faintly heroic character the public craved. He had something of the Everyman about him. At Eagle Rock, his mailbox was fit to burst some mornings. The *Everybody's* interview was picked up across America and beyond. Newspapers from Chicago to Brisbane carried almost-identical versions of the story.

The more famous Hatfield became, the more fevered his old adversaries at the weather bureau grew in their efforts to discredit him. When Paul, back from France, visited the Los Angeles Weather Bureau in U.S. Army uniform and obtained rainfall figures and other weather reports, complaints were made to the weather bureau's new chief, Charles Marvin. Should the bureau be helping anyone—even a war veteran—a letter to Marvin in 1918 asked, "when we know that such data is to be used in fraudulent practices?" Marvin worked hard to undermine the Hatfield brothers, but like Willis Moore before him, he discovered that Hollywood saw that there's no such thing as bad publicity.

The *Everybody's* piece stirred enough interest in Alberta, Canada, for Charles to receive an invitation from the Lethbridge Board of Trade. Before committing to a contract the civic group asked the U.S. Weather Bureau for its opinion of the rainmaker. Charles Marvin's response was so damning that the Canadians not only dropped the idea of hiring Charles but published Marvin's comments in local newspapers and then published them as a pamphlet. Farmers were advised that they should put their hard-earned cash into irrigation schemes rather than "a big lumber stand" with "some washing soda on top."

There were still plenty of people who believed in Charles more than they believed in any Washington bureaucrat or self-appointed civic leader, however. Just one hundred miles to the east of Lethbridge, the community of Medicine Hat was in the grip of a five-year drought. To them Charles's business card, by now complete with pictures of his towers in place, was a symbol of hope. They ignored their colleagues in Lethbridge and hired him for a season.

The Medicine Hat contract turned into one of the highlights of Charles's career. Within days, reports of heavy rainfall were coming in from all over the region. On May 16, 1921, the United Agricultural Association received a telegram from a farmer. It read:

RAIN ENOUGH. STOP FOR A FEW DAYS.

Charles found his tower inundated with visitors. A moviemaker tried to film him. Charles wasn't ready to have his operation paraded on the *Movietone* news bulletins and gave the filmmaker short shrift.

Buoyed by the attention, Charles intimated—as he had done before—that his secret was so important it "should never be in private hands." "It is a work that should be controlled by government regulation, he told a newspaper in Sheridan, Wyoming, that summer, "for the results obtained are so great and the influences spread over such a vast territory that the handling of these important operations, especially in years of drought, is far too great a responsibility for any individual shoulders to bear."

THE DETROIT NEWS, SUNDAY, MAY 15, 1921
'Rainmaker' Gets Results, Breaking 5-Year Drought

Just the medicine. A Detroit newspaper reports Hatfield's success in Medicine Hat, Alberta. Detroit News, Sunday, May 15, 1921.

Fred Binney began to lobby for Charles to be given a job by Congress. He circulated a letter to newspapers in which he argued Washington should buy the Hatfield formula, give him an annuity of $24,000, and get the Division of Forestry to construct a network of rainmaking towers across the West. Binney blamed "three men in a Washington Bureau" for "blocking the way to this grand result" and said he did not need to name names.

Fred Binney's relentless promotion of rainmaking as a science came to an abrupt end on December 5, 1927, at San Diego's County Hospital. He died as convinced as ever about the possibilities of scientific rainmaking. But he also passed away unaware of the events of July and August 1922, and the most intriguing "success" of Charles Hatfield's career.

Hatfield had become unhappy with his existing formula and wanted to try a different approach "solely from a private standpoint." He took his equipment to one of the most remote spots in the state, Sand Canyon, at Black Mountain on the edge of the Mojave Desert, twenty-five miles northwest of Randsburg, where he erected a six-foot tower and began operations at 7:30 A.M. on Wednesday, July 26.

As ever, the exact details of his formula remained a secret. However, it is the only one of his experiments for which his diary notes survive. According to Charles's log, when he began work there were "no visible clouds in sight, it being clear—positively so."

By the following day, "a few cirrus clouds" could be observed here and there. That afternoon "to the S.E. some large Cumulus formation had appeared."

The cloud continued to build up until Sunday, when, "as the day advanced, Cumulus formed in all directions. . . . Light sprinkles falling at 9:30 P.M."

The rain returned at 3 P.M. on Monday "and so continued until 7:00 A.M. in which time 1.15 inches precipitated itself." On Monday evening Charles reported "a few flashes of lightning to the South."

By Tuesday, eight days into his experiment, "gigantic Cumulus clouds were growing to immense proportions. . . . As night came on they came together and were accompanied with vivid flashes of lightning which continued for an hour or more, and an immense rainfall occurred at the head of Sand Canyon of cloudburst proportions."

Charles's brief notes fail to capture the power or the effect of this "cloudburst."

There was an independent witness. Joe Lacey looked after the Kern County Aqueduct for the Los Angeles Water Department and lived with his wife and children in the shadow of the mountains. Lacey had witnessed thunderstorms before, so at first thought little of it when he saw the telltale signs gathering that evening. But he soon understood the scale of the storm that was being unleashed.

"At about 9 o'clock that evening the thunder became unusually violent. I could see the flashes of lightning and when the flashes came I could see the great black clouds piled up like mountains over the top of Sand Canyon."

When he heard what sounded like a truck approaching he initially thought it must be two nearby homesteaders. "The noise began to sound like several motor trucks. Then it sounded like 100 trucks and then like about 1,000 freight trains." A wall of water was coming down the canyon. He ran back to the house and managed to get a call through to the water department before rushing his family to higher ground. "I told them that Sand Canyon was about to be washed off the face of the earth."

Lacey ran to join his family in the hills, then watched in awe as "the torrent of water, brush, boulders, and trees thundered past, surging and tumbling down the canyon as if the Amazon River had been turned loose in it." The rains continued until 4:00 A.M. It was not until first light that he saw the extent of the damage. By then a team from the water department had arrived to assess the damage. Miraculously, the aqueduct had survived. But little else had.

Lacey's home was swept away in a sea of black silt. The silt spread out across several miles and extended into the desert for fifteen miles. The damage in the canyons was even more severe. The area was inaccessible for days. The first group through included a man named John Hogg, a contributor to *Popular Science*. The scene provided him with one of the biggest stories of his career.

Hogg was awestruck by the sea of debris that had flowed into the desert. "Simply untold millions of tons of earth and debris" had been released in what he called "one of the most extraordinary freak storms ever staged in the terrestrial drama." The previous day the canyon had been filled with deer, bears, and four square miles of towering pines. Now it was "a bottomless deposit of thick, black mud, strewn with logs, brush and boulders." The canyon looked like it had been "blasted by a flow of lava from some titanic volcanic upheaval" with "holes that looked like the work of dynamite blasts where the rain had dug the soil away.

"It took somewhat of a stretch of the imagination to visualize what the downpour must have been like while it lasted," Hogg's report ended. "But from the evidence it left on the landscape, Shakespeare's tempest must have been a sort of San Francisco fog compared with it."

In his detailed article on the freak storm, however, Hogg deprived the readers of *Popular Science* of one detail. Neither he nor Lacey knew it, but high above the devastated desert gorges, Charles and Paul slept out the storm that night. The following afternoon they took down their camp, erased all evidence of having been there, and headed home quietly.

Hatfield's name was never associated with the storm.

Charles's reasons for keeping quiet are unclear. In the wake of San Diego, he may have feared finding himself at the wrong end of a lawsuit. More likely, however, he was becoming resigned to his status in the mind of the public and the scientific establishment.

Big-city newspapers loved portraying Hatfield and his back-woods clients as participants in a series of comedies straight from the Mack Sennett studios. In 1924 the Los Angeles press had a field day with a contract in the San Joaquin Valley, at Coalinga. Hatfield set up his towers in March. Reporters joked about how his "Tower of Showers" was ready to start the work of "Tickling the Clouds to Tears." Sure enough Charles persuaded "J Pluvius to turn on the celestial sprinkling cart" and it "rained little fishes." The newspapers claimed Hatfield's tent was washed away by a cloudburst and that he and Paul were forced to spend a night in a tree before the floodwaters subsided. Paul denied this ever happened. Charles simply collected his prize. The *Los Angeles Herald* pictured him "wearing his $8,000 smile."

The image some had of Hatfield as a fast-talking huckster preying on slow-witted farmers was certainly misplaced. His back-country clients did their best to outwit him in their contracts, and at times the lessons of San Diego still went unheeded. A deal struck near Bakersfield, California, in December 1924 tripped Charles up not once but twice. He had offered the first inch for free and was horrified when the farmer's rain gauges showed the rainfall for the month at 0.9 inch. His own rain gauge showed 3 inches. He accused them of placing one of their gauges in "one of the driest spots in the desert." He also kicked himself for offering the first inch of rain for free when he knew the average for the area was just over 0.5 inch in December. He put it down to experience. "The mistake I made was in the contract and the choosing of the gauges," he said. However, he never considered a job a failure: "When I went up there the sheep and cattle men were desperate. There was not a blade of green grass in sight. Everything was brown and pasturage was nil. When I left last week the grass was several inches high. The valleys were green and there is pasturage for several months. Would you call that a failure?"

Yet he continued to work, outlasting every new rainmaking prodigy who cropped up. Farmers remained his most loyal defenders.

In Fresno in 1924, Hatfield claimed the second-heaviest rainfall in his contracting life. "There are lots of farmers convinced Hatfield can do all he says he does," said one local wheat farmer. "I claim the investment with Hatfield was a pretty good one. The seed was dormant until we had these rains, which did not come until after Hatfield had begun his operations. We had .3 inches of rain in the lake bottoms up to the time Hatfield came. The weather bureau knows this but they won't admit it." It is a testament to Charles that twenty years after he went into the business he could still find men to voice such unyielding trust in him— and such scorn for the weather bureau.

Such conviction was hard to ignore. Yet there were still those who shared the ambivalence captured in a piece in the *Los Angeles Sunday Times* that March. Two decades after the boy wizard had emerged to break the great drought, Los Angelenos still weren't sure what to make of him. "Some think Hatfield is merely a great showman; others something else less complimentary, but some, and always enough for his purposes, think him a man ahead of his time, who can do what the United States Weather Bureau and all modern science say is impossible."

Hatfield's dream of clearing London's fog never materialized, but overseas adventures of a more modest kind eventually came his way. The publicity generated by his success at Medicine Hat aroused the interest of larger agricultural bodies.

In 1925, the American Sugar Cane League was on the verge of signing a contract to pay $8,000 for two inches of rain in

Louisiana. This time Charles's cause was undermined by Isaac Cline, the ill-fated weather forecaster from the Galveston disaster of 1900. Now head of the New Orleans Weather Bureau, Cline used ninety years of statistics to argue that two inches of rain in May was below the average. He accused Hatfield of being a good player of percentages. "A man can bet on two inches of rain during the month of May for a considerable period and he will win about 75 per cent of the time," he said. The contract was never signed, but Charles's blend of charisma and conviction had too many admirers for the weather bureau to keep up.

He would soon receive inquiries from such far-flung locations as Cuba, Tunis, Panama, and Colombia. Like the contract in Louisiana, none of these hardened into firm commissions.

Yet such was the press's infatuation with Hatfield that tales of amazing overseas adventures emerged anyway. In 1922, reports surfaced that he was in Naples helping the Italian government break a lengthy drought. He was supposedly planning to meet Pope Pius XI and water the Vatican's gardens. After a few weeks, newspapers reported, "all Southern Italy was flooded." Farmers went "wild with joy" and the rainmaker became "a bigger hero than Mussolini."

"We were never there," Paul said later. However, they were, definitely in Honduras.

In the summer of 1929, Hatfield received an urgent wire from the Standard Steamship and Fruit Company in New Orleans. A fire was threatening its 100,000-banana plantation in Honduras. It wanted Charles to travel to South America to tackle the blaze.

Charles agreed to spend ten days there. He signed a contract for $1,500 to put out the fire. He and Paul caught the Sunset Limited to New Orleans, where their new employers had held their cargo ship in anticipation of the brothers' arrival. The journey through the Gulf of Mexico and the Straits of Yucatan ended at the port of La Ceiba. When they arrived at the plantation, the manager greeted them with something close to contempt. "He thought we were freaks," Paul recalled. After three days, the skies turned purple. "Oh my," Paul said. "It just poured, lightning and thunder."

Charles provided his own version of events: "A dozen huge magnolia and mahogany trees were struck and knocked down by lightning within 500 feet of my rain tower. A small building thirty feet from the tower was struck and part of its roof torn off." The storm sent the locals into a frenzy. "Their wonderment over my apparatus turned to wholesale terror."

Hatfield returned to Eagle Rock in June 1930 to find newspapers once again hanging on his every word. In Seattle, readers of the *Post-Intelligencer* were served up a colorful account of the Honduras episode. The headline read: WHEN YOU EAT A BANANA, THINK OF CHARLES M. HATFIELD . . . WHO CLAIMS HE SAVED THE HONDURAS CROP WHILE LIGHTNING FLASHED AND NATIVES WAILED.

The Honduran plantation invited Charles and Paul again the following year, and again they produced rain. Charles's dreams of an international reputation stirred within him once more. This time his personal life proved his undoing. Charles returned to Eagle Rock to find that Mable had served him with divorce papers.

In a life overcrowded with secrets, Hatfield's marriage to Mable had remained the most mysterious element of all. In the acres of newsprint devoted to Charles's exploits, she had not merited a single mention. Neither had his two stepchildren.

Mrs. Hatfield emerged from the shadows on March 25, 1931. That day the *San Diego Union* carried a report of the divorce settlement she had won in the Los Angeles courts. Apparently the marriage had been over for some time. Mable was unhappy with the financial arrangements and had gone to court in the wake of the Honduras expedition. She claimed Charles had pocketed $10,000 on his second visit to Central America. Charles denied it.

The court favored Mable, ordering a division of their property and an alimony payment of $7 a week. As with so many aspects of Charles's life, the incident raised more questions than it answered.

Divorce marked the personal low point of Charles's life. Afterward he suffered bouts of melancholia and heart trouble. Mable died in 1935, four years after their divorce, at the age of just fifty-four. He remained estranged from his stepchildren Richard and Leila.

The demise of the rainmaking business didn't help his spirits. Although the economic depression produced a miniature revival in the form of a new wave of rainmaking bombardiers, by the mid-1930s the completion of the most ambitious of the southwest's irrigation projects, the Boulder Dam, signaled the final curtain for the last of the old rainmakers. The Boulder Dam diverted the Colorado River and supplied water to half of Southern California, including Los Angeles and San Diego.

Hatfield reverted to selling sewing machines and had a tilt at his father's old passion, selling real estate. After the pain of his divorce, he found a glimmer of happiness when he rediscovered an old love, Martha McLain. They married in 1937.

As the depression dragged on and the worst dust-bowl drought in memory hit the historic birthplace of rainmaking, schemes to resurrect Hatfield popped up every now and again. The *Kansas City Star* ran a campaign to get him on the job. President Franklin Roosevelt was urged to bring him out of semi-retirement. "Six to eight of his towers set up in Kansas or Nebraska should do the trick," observed the *Star*. But by the outbreak of World War II, his rainmaking days were over. At Eagle Rock, he readied himself for retirement, for long days leafing through his scrapbooks and his gradual disappearance into the backwaters of American history.

THE RAINMAKER

O n October 28, 1954, New York's Cort Theater staged the premiere of *The Rainmaker*, a new play by N. Richard Nash. Nash's drama was set "in a western state on a summer day in a time of drought" and centered on Lizzie Curry, played that night by Geraldine Page. Lizzie was a lonely spinster living with her father and two brothers. Her siblings were trying (unsuccessfully) to fix her up with a husband when a mysterious rainmaker, Starbuck, appeared one night, offering to produce rain and threatening to sweep Lizzie off her feet at the same time. Was he a con man out to exploit Lizzie and the farmers? Or was he the man to bring rain and simultaneously lift the metaphorical drought that was Lizzie's loveless life? The play was an immediate hit. By 1956 Hollywood was making the film, starring Katharine Hepburn and Burt Lancaster.

The film's Los Angeles premiere was held on December 18 of that year. The studio, Paramount, had considered sending a plane to drop dry ice in the clouds, but balked at the $10,000 fee. Publicist Rufus Blair came up with the obvious alternative.

In interviews, Nash said his play was inspired by a boyhood fascination with the exploits of the West's famous rainmakers, and Charles Hatfield in particular. "I tried to tell a simple story about droughts that happen to people, and about faith," Nash said. The studio publicists sensed a perfect opportunity and wheeled out America's preeminent rain wizard.

Their instincts were sound. By the 1950s, Hatfield's place in the legend of Southern California had taken on an air of permanence —not to mention a slightly surreal edge. Radio stations, newspapers, and even state officials had begun to routinely connect his appearance in their offices with outbreaks of rain.

When he was divorced from Mable, the judge, noticing it was raining outside, made a dry remark along the lines of: "I hope this is not a sign of Mr. Hatfield's displeasure with us." When he and Martha arrived in San Francisco on honeymoon, a local newspaper couldn't resist picking up on the fact that it started raining at the same time. Los Angeles newspapers seemed to genuinely believe in a link. "There is a tradition regarding Hatfield," reported the *LA Evening Herald and Express*, in 1942, "often after his name is mentioned or his picture appears in this newspaper there is a weather disturbance." The paper had run a picture of Charles in advance of his being interviewed on local radio station KFAC. "The government has permitted it to be known that the rain fell in Los Angeles last Saturday—nearly an inch," the paper said. "Thus continuing the precedent."

The man behind the legend was something of a disappointment. Now in his eighties, Hatfield was suffering from heart problems. Martha had died earlier that year. He looked frail and faintly bemused as he turned up for the Hollywood premiere. At the publicist's request he indulged in staged playfulness with the film's second leads, Earl Holliman and Yvonne Lime. Photographs of him standing outside the theater holding an umbrella over the pair flashed their way across the country. It didn't rain, however.

The film brought renewed media attention. At Eagle Rock, attempts to winkle his formula out of him proved as fruitless as ever. "That's my secret. I may pass it on later, but I won't tell it now," he said in 1957. Inevitably, the interviews always ended in San Diego in 1916.

He was still defiant. "The rain of 1916 was an act of Hatfield, not an act of God," he said. The old bitterness had become something more akin to sadness. One interviewer who made the trek to Eagle Rock described how Charles had been talkative until San Diego came up. "The old rainmaker grew quiet at this point in his narrative."

"I never got a nickel," he said eventually. "To this day I've never felt right about that San Diego City Council."

Such was the renewed interest that a television company made an afternoon play about the events of January 1916. It was a colorful, semicomic drama in the vein of the many magazine articles that had been written about Hatfield and San Diego over the years.

"Charles loved it," said Paul.

Nash's play spun off into a musical, *110 Degrees in the Shade*. But it was the original stage version that endured.

In 1999, the year before Nash's death, the play became a hit again, revived on Broadway with Woody Harrelson as Starbuck opposite Jayne Atkinson as Lizzie. Its success underlined its status as a small classic, a seminal American fable about hope and the conflict between realists and dreamers.

Faith was a quality Starbuck's prototype had in abundance. "There is one person who believes in Hatfield and his ability with all his heart and soul, and that person is Hatfield himself. No one can talk with him ten minutes without being thoroughly convinced of his sincerity and his faith in his system," one interviewer wrote of Charles in 1924.

He took that faith with him to his grave.

Charles died at home in Eagle Rock on January 12, 1958. Even his passing fed the legend. Charles had insisted his death be kept a secret. Paul complied and oversaw a private burial at Forest Lawn Cemetery. Only Paul, his second wife Lilian, a priest, and a representative from the undertakers were present. No public announcement was made.

Paul managed to keep a lid on the story for three months. Inevitably, in mid-April, the news leaked out. Even the *New York Times* ran an obituary. In California, newspapers thought the moment significant enough to justify a comment in the lead columns. The fame Charles had yearned for in life was bestowed on him in death.

On April 18, the *San Diego Evening Tribune* ran an editorial. "He trained no one in the magic art that some say nearly washed San Diego into the sea. Whatever special skills and knowledge he may have possessed seem to have departed with him—a sorry fact to report. In a way it is as though Pasteur or Dr. Salk had refused to let humanity know the secrets of their great discoveries."

Another encomium began: "When the historians are making up a list of the nation's most forgotten men, we trust they won't overlook the name of Charles Mallory Hatfield."

"PROFESSOR" HATFIELD'S STORM?

I n the nine decades since San Diego's strangest meteorological
month, the flood of people eager to explain what really happened in January 1916 has slowed to a gentle stream.

The weather bureau's guesswork in 1916 satisfied few people.
But neither did Hatfield's faith-based claim. For most San Diegans, the courts' definition seemed the easiest way to draw a veil
over the episode. It had been an Act of God rather than an "Act
of Hatfield," as Charles liked to put it. But this didn't satisfy
everyone.

For a period, the argument centered on Hatfield himself. The
president of Stanford University, David Starr Jordan, delivered
a blow in 1925 when he invented a new word to describe the
art Charles practiced. He called it "pluviculture" and placed it

in the same category as astrology and palm reading. Jordan dismissed the movement as "sciosophy" practiced by what he called a breed of "quacktitioner." His ideas received a wide airing in California.

Throughout this time, the professional weathermen conducted their own parallel argument. At the Federal Building, and then at the San Diego Weather Bureau's office at Lindbergh Field, Dean Blake would grow to become a national figure, known as the "flying weatherman" for his pioneering work in using aerial observations for forecasting. He was such good friends with Charles Lindbergh that the aviator would call Blake for a personal weather forecast every evening after supper.

In August 1933, Blake was instrumental in compiling the most extensive study of the region's weather ever published in the *Monthly Weather Review*. The report confirmed the complexity of San Diego's weather and identified four types of storms as the sources of the region's rainfall: North Pacifics, South Pacifics, Interiors, and Mexicans.

Of the four, the North Pacifics were the most common cause of rain. The storms, which tended to swing southeastward from Alaska between November and May, contributed 43 percent of San Diego's rain and tended to be the most regular. The South Pacific storms, emerging from the Pacific between San Francisco and the Tropic of Cancer, were much more irregular and produced about 19 percent of San Diego's rain, most of it of a warmer and heavier variety. Interior storms were much more erratic and occurred mostly during spring. They accounted for 30 percent of the city's rain. Finally, the Mexican storms were the rarest but often the most spectacular. They accounted for much of the rain in the mountain areas and were cited as the source of the region's greatest cloudburst on record, at Campo in 1891, when 11.5 inches of rain fell in 80 minutes.

The report underlined Blake's growing opinion that three storms had hit San Diego in 1916—not two, as the weather bureau claimed originally. "There were three of them, if I remember rightly, and following very closely." His reputation was such that this became the accepted theory for thirty years.

Blake's theories about San Diego's smog being inherited from Los Angeles and the region's weather conforming to a ten-year wet cycle also became widely accepted. He retired shortly after completing fifty years service in 1952. On two subjects, however, he remained unclear until his death. One was whether San Diego would ever be able to protect itself from storms of the kind that blew in from the Pacific, or Mexico, in the last week of January 1916. The other was rainmaking.

To a man with Blake's length of service, it must have been an extraordinary moment when he was asked by the weather bureau to oversee a rainmaking program that it was sanctioning.

The tests were run by the San Diego Weather Modification Company in the 1940s and were instigated in the wake of the remarkable breakthroughs being made at the time. In 1946, Vincent Schaefer, a scientist with General Electric, took off in a plane over Schenectady, New York, guided the pilot east to a bank of gray rain clouds, and scattered three pounds of dry ice into the atmosphere.

Minutes later, several thousand feet below, Schaefer's mentor, Nobel laureate Irving Langmuir, reported flakes of snow falling. "We did it," Schaefer shouted through his radio. Scientific rainmaking had become a reality.

The roots of their triumph stretched all the way back to 1891, Chicago, and rocket maker Louis Gathmann's idea of releasing carbonic acid gas into clouds. Gathmann's idea was scientifically sound. Cooling clouds to subzero temperatures was at least half the key to the rainmaking riddle. But it was more than fifty years before anyone found an agent capable of cooling clouds with the accuracy and intensity needed.

Schaefer's and Langmuir's success in 1946 revived interest in rainmaking. Two schools of cloud seeding emerged—warm and cold. The former, inspired by Lucien Blake's sawdust and turpentine "smoke balls" in the 1890s, used salt crystals, superheated sand, urea, and ammonium sulphate as artificial-condensation nuclei. The latter used supercoolants to speed up the formation of ice crystals.

From Charles Hatfield's point of view, the experiment Langmuir conducted three years later, in 1949, was the most significant. In Santa Fe, Langmuir began testing the properties of silver iodide, another cloud-manipulating agent. He arranged a line of generators that burned a chemical combination, a mixture of silver iodide, acetone, and propane. Langmuir found that he could turn rain off and on "at will" simply by turning the generators on and off. Suddenly, the "moisture accelerator's" experiments didn't seem so outlandish after all.

In San Diego, Dean Blake smelled a rat. "The amount of rain claimed was not the amount that the figures showed fell," he said.

Yet as cloud seeding struggled for acceptance, Blake foresaw a day when artificial rain would fall on San Diego. "Some day a way to change the weather may be found," he said in 1962. "Of course, in precipitation there's certainly enough water vapor in the air, but at present, controlling it is not feasible."

Blake's view of the 1916 storm was eventually challenged. In 1961, San Diego State University meteorologist Dr. Don Edemiller claimed no less than four weather fronts collided to cause the devastation. He based his case on World War II weather maps that re-created infamous weather according to modern air-mass analysis.

Edemiller argued that in January 1916, the "Pacific High" that normally protects Southern California from northwestern rains had moved 10 degrees south. Four distinct storms formed during the month and the area of low pressure over Southern California sucked in each of them. As the quartet collided, air of different temperatures came together at their leading edges. A pinwheel effect produced San Diego's answer to the perfect storm, generating the cloudbursts that soaked the region.

Edemiller used Hatfield as a way to publicize his conclusions.

As far as San Diego newspapers were concerned, his analysis became the definitive proof that Hatfield's Flood was misnamed. Edemiller chose to overlook the large body of evidence that proved small-scale, ground-based cloud seeding could be effective. He also ignored Charles's fateful statements in February 1916, disclaiming himself as the source of the entire West Coast weather system.

Instead, Edemiller used the fact that record-breaking weather was happening elsewhere to argue Charles could not possibly have been responsible. Oregon had record levels of snow, as did Idaho, while Nevada and Arizona experienced their wettest months since records began being kept in 1892.

"If you believe that Hatfield caused the rain in San Diego," Edemiller argued, "you also have to believe that the influence of that smoke rearranged the distribution of air masses as far north as Alaska, at least a third of the way across the Pacific Ocean and as far east as the Great Plains.

"Hatfield boasted his system worked to bring the clouds over San Diego. To have supplied enough energy to produce weather patterns such as occurred in January 1916 would have taken several hundred hydrogen bombs."

Even to those romantics in love with the idea of the legend of San Diego's rainmaker, Edemiller seemed to close the door on Charles's claims for good. But late-twentieth-century science allowed them to nudge that door open once more.

In the age of the satellite and the supercomputer, the scientific establishment's view of rainmaking remains as divided as it was in the days of Frank Melbourne, Willis Moore, and the old weather bureau. The most comprehensive review of modern cloud seeding, published in the *Bulletin of the American Meteorological Society* in 1999, considered all the studies conducted in recent years and came up with a blend of good and bad news. Its author, R. T. Bruintjes, pored over the numerous experiments conducted not just in America, but in Africa and Australia and elsewhere. He concluded that there was "considerable skepticism" about whether "glaciogenic" seeding, of the dry-ice kind pioneered by Schaefer, "provides a cost-effective means for increasing precipitation." But at the same time he concluded that "hygroscopic" seeding, the so-called warm-air cloud seeding using salt, ammonium sulphate, and other agents, "provided for renewed optimism." In other words, after more than half a century of experimenting, the jury was still out.

If the conclusions of another influential study are to be believed, that jury may remain out for a very long time. The report, published in the *Journal of Applied Meteorology* in 1995, looked at the much-manipulated skies above Lake Almanor, California, in the fourteen years between 1978 and 1992. There was no doubt that seeding with silver iodide had produced small but significant amounts of snow in the area. But the silver-traced snow had fallen in such a haphazard and diffuse pattern—often far from the "target area"—it was impossible to draw hard conclusions, except for one. The study concluded that the general unpredictability of the atmosphere, and low-level winds in particular, made it difficult to measure the effectiveness of cloud seeding with any statistical accuracy. In essence, it admitted that twenty-first-century scientists will continue to be frustrated by the problems that plagued James Espy and his nineteenth-century counterparts. The atmosphere is simply too vast, complex, and unpredictable to prove anything for certain.

It is unsurprising then that, for many, the most persuasive arguments about the atmosphere now lie in "nonlinear dynamics," so-called chaos theory, and the famous "butterfly" analogy.

Chaos theory's founder was Konrad Lorenz. But it was Ernest Zebrowski, Jr. who put the central argument best in his book *Perils of a Restless Planet.* Zebrowski was analyzing the origins of hurricanes when he asked: "Suppose that a tropical storm develops and that we play back the data record of the previous few days. What do we find as we go back in time? A smaller storm, and yet a smaller disturbance, then a warm moist windy spot, then a set of atmospheric conditions that looks no different from that at many other locations in the tropics."

Zebrowski applied Lorenz's framework to wonder: "Could a butterfly in a West African rain forest, by flitting to the left of a tree rather than to the right, possibly set into motion a chain of events that escalates into a hurricane striking coastal South Carolina a few weeks later?"

Zebrowski observed that while all hurricanes have common characteristics, such as thunderstorms, computer models show that tiny differences in conditions during the formation of a storm produce immense variations in the magnitude of the fully formed hurricane.

"Add a little glitch," Zebrowski wrote, "a metaphorical butterfly, to a complex process, and sometimes you get an outcome no rational person would ever have expected."

For those in search of definitive answers, it is a difficult concept to embrace. But if the last century and a half of meteorological science has revealed anything, it is that definitive answers are not available. They are certainly not available when it comes to the events of January 1916. No one knows what Charles Hatfield let loose in the skies above Lake Morena. No one knows for certain where the storm or storms—however many of them they were—formed before unleashing themselves on San Diego and its surrounding countryside. There is no question the storms were widespread across the West Coast. But nowhere were the effects so catastrophic—and not just on man-made constructions —as they were in San Diego and its surrounding countryside. Why was that?

So Zebrowski's elegant argument raises one final tantalizing possibility. It may not have required the force of "several hundred hydrogen bombs" to destabilize the skies above Morena. Perhaps Charles Hatfield was simply the metaphorical "butterfly" that complicated the already-complex processes at work in the Southern Californian atmosphere. Maybe, just maybe, his mysterious "rain stew" triggered the "little glitch" that transformed itself into a storm that almost destroyed a city and its dreams.

We can never know.

HATFIELD THE RAINMAKER
[San Diego, 2005]

I n contemporary San Diego, the story of Charles Hatfield is
remembered with a blend of warmth and mild embarrassment
that echoes the feelings of the city's forefathers. The story of
Hatfield's Flood is too good to be airbrushed out of the city's
history. At the same time the events of January 1916 are remembered wryly, dryly—and discreetly.

The one permanent memorial to the city's notorious rainmaker stands on the roadside just off Interstate 8, at the junction
of Buckman Springs Road and Oak Road, a mile or so from
Lake Morena and the park that now surrounds it. It is a plaque,
bolted to a simple red granite pedestal, first erected in 1973 by
the Native Sons of the Golden West. The original plaque was
defaced and removed, but it was replaced again in 1987, this time

with an inscription that explained its incongruous presence in this still-remote spot.

Couched in the careful, legally correct language of another age, the wording leaves more unsaid than revealed. In this sense, at least, it seems a fitting tribute. It reads:

Hatfield the Rainmaker

Charles M. Hatfield offered to fill Lake Morena to over-flowing for $10,000. To avert a serious water shortage the City of San Diego voted to accept his offer but failed to sign the contract. In early January 1916 Hatfield and brother Paul erected towers east of Morena and began releasing chemicals. On January 14 rain began falling totaling 35 inches. On January 27 lower Otay Dam burst and a wing of Sweetwater Dam broke. The flood caused damage over $3 ½ million. San Diego refused to pay Hatfield declaring the rain "an act of God." Hatfield filed a law suit to no avail. He quietly left the area.

The only other remnant of Hatfield's story lies under lock and key in the vaults beneath the city's main library.

With his brother's passing, Paul became the custodian of the secret formula. Predictably he treated it with all the protectiveness he had shown his big brother. He talked of picking up the torch himself but was prevented by a California statute introduced in 1951 and amended regularly through the 1950s that required rainmakers to be licensed. The original statute simply required all rainmakers to have a $50 permit. "That was all right," said Paul. "Then when he starts the operation he has to tell everything he uses. That killed it right there."

Paul Hatfield died in 1974, but before his death he turned up unannounced at the library with a selection of scrapbooks and a box containing some of Charles's rainmaking gear. At first glance, the modest instruments seem an uninspiring, mildly baffling collection of semiscientific bric-a-brac.

They include a battered barometer, a rusted rain gauge, a set of scales, and a box of weights. The measuring stick is a school ruler, split in half.

Then one detail catches the eye.

Throughout his eventful life as a moisture accelerator, Charles Hatfield kept his burnished brass barometer close. It was his early-warning system when he arrived in San Diego in December 1915 and remained his key weather-predicting tool until he retired. A testament to the craft of its makers, the barometer's precision-balanced inner workings are pristine; its coils, springs, and needles gleam as if new.

Only on the outside does its weather-weary past reveal itself. The barometer's glass is soiled and misted in parts so as to leave the filigreed markings—Stormy, Rain, Change, Fair, Very Dry— faint, broken, and hard to read. It is difficult to say what might have caused the damage—wear and tear, exposure, perhaps—but it is obvious that one quadrant received the most wear over the years. Naturally, it is the one around Stormy and Rain.

ACKNOWLEDGMENTS

There is a world of difference between writing the story of great events and the giant figures who created them and telling an overlooked tale at whose heart sits an enigma. If I had chosen to write a book about Charles Hatfield's heroes—James Espy and the scientists at the heart of the Great Law of Storms debate, for instance, or even Luther Burbank—I could have drawn on libraries laden with diaries and correspondence, official papers, and scientific journals. But I didn't. Instead I chose the shadow-figure that was Charles Hatfield.

The great rainmaker would, I'm certain, have been annoyed even to discover that his mother's scrapbook and a few odd pieces of correspondence survived him. He wouldn't have appreciated his brother Paul's talkativeness in the later years of his life, and

261

the flesh his frequent interviews would allow someone like me to add to the bare bones of his story. Charles Hatfield left no memoirs, no detailed notes of his experiments, few notes of any kind in fact. The caginess he displayed in life—and, vicariously, in death—was, I suspect, less a device to protect his privacy than a policy designed to enhance his professional persona, to protect the essential mystery that he traded upon. Rather like an actor, Hatfield enjoyed being well known but did not want people to know him too well. It was an act he cultivated with skill, and as I set out to tell this story it presented me with my greatest challenge: How to fill in the gaping holes created by Hatfield's elusive nature?

I have been scrupulous to the point of pedantry on the central facts of this story; dates, deaths, times, temperatures, places, people, rainfall and runoff figures are all drawn from the official record. In drawing and delineating Charles Hatfield's inner life I have been equally scrupulous, never straying from the public record, his public utterances, and quotes from those who knew him well. Only in expanding the narrative to re-create the sights, smells, and feelings of the people involved in the tumultuous events of January 1916 did I draw on deduction, detective work, and, ultimately, my imagination.

In both aspects I was fortunate to be able to draw inspiration from a mass of material, provided by a group of people to whom I am hugely indebted. In San Diego, Jane Selvar and the staff of the California Room at the San Diego City Library opened up their Hatfield Collection and with it a window into the rainmaker's world.

My job here was made all the easier by a past member of the library, Marion L. Buckner, who did invaluable work in indexing the piles of Hatfield ephemera in their collection. In a note from April of 1969, Ms. Buckner expressed her hope that "perhaps some day, these papers . . . will give someone an opportunity to reevaluate and publicize the lifelong endeavors of Charles Mallory Hatfield, San Diego's famous rainmaker." Throughout the writing of this book I was all too aware of how important an opportunity it was, and I hope I have seized it. Of the current members of the library, I would like to thank Jane and Rick Crawford in particular, not least for letting me "play" with the curious collection of moisture-accelerating ephemera that makes up the Hatfield instrument collection. Holding his weather-beaten barometer in my hands was a strangely stirring experience.

The San Diego Historical Society's reputation extends to London, where, long before I traveled to California, I was told it was among the best if not *the* best historical society in America. I saw nothing to persuade me otherwise during my visit there.

The society's collection of oral histories, contemporaneous letters, and diaries proved a treasure trove of reminiscences about the flood and its effects on people's lives. The recollections of people like Dean Blake, Seymour Tulloch, Rose Dysart, and Emmanuelle Daneri were indispensable. The society's collection of photographs evokes the period perfectly, too. Here as everywhere, everyone was a model of patience and helpfulness, but I must single out Dennis Sharp, who lived up to his surname with the precision and speed with which he accommodated my requests. Thanks must also go to Bob Witty, John Panter, and Chris Myers.

As research gave way to writing, I was able to fall back on the support of others. From the outset, Dr. Steve LeComber of Queen Mary's College at the University of London was an enthusiastic adviser cum motivator, a ready provider of scientific skepticism and editing sense. Elsewhere I am indebted to Wayne Donaldson and the staffs of the Los Angeles Times Library, the Los Angeles Public Library, and the British Science Library, where—thanks to a curious piece of good fortune—I found the most detailed records of Seth Swenson's daily water measurements at Morena in the U.S. Geological Surveys held there.

The most heartfelt thanks must be reserved for four people, however. It was my greatest good fortune to find Jofie Ferrari-Adler, my editor at Thunder's Mouth Press. His enthusiasm for the story—and my ideas about how best to tell it—nudged me to the finish line that was the first draft. From there his expert eye for narrative clarity improved subsequent drafts enormously.

Inevitably, it was my family who played the other key role. My wife Cilene provided the initial encouragement for me to take what was something of a gamble on my behalf. Her simple message, "go for it," meant much more than she realized at the time. My young children Thomas and Gabriella provided subtler support, Thomas with his regular visits to my office to drag me out for a coffee, Gabriella with her fascinated reaction when I first outlined the story of what she came to call "the man who made the rain." Her words were as encouraging as any I encountered during the long journey that led to the completion of this book. So it is to her—along with her brother and mother—that I dedicate it.

SOURCES

Collections

The Hatfield Papers, Volumes I–IV, San Diego Public Library.

The Hatfield Scrapbooks, Volumes 1 and 2, Los Angeles Central Public Library.

Oral Histories held at the San Diego Public Library

Hatfield, Paul. "The Hatfield Brothers, Rainmakers," UCLA Oral History Program, 1972.

Oral Histories held at the San Diego Historical Society

Daisy Abell, Mary Addis, Leonora Alvarado, Carrie Ambler, John L. Bacon, Gerald Baldwin, Helen Baranov, Dean Blake, Ray Bond, Edgar Cooper, Aurelia De Bincenzi Daneri, Grace Diffendorf, Ed Fletcher, Helen Gute, Harry Haelsig, Clarence Harris, Paul Hatch, Robert Holmes, Alonzo Jessop, James Russell Johnson, Walter M. Johnson, Dr. J. Knox, Daisy Leahy, Katherine Nicholson Leng, E. G. Martin, Charles Moore, Vibert Mossholder, Newell Jacob Peavey, Clarence Rand, Nathan Louis Rannells, Roy Saum, Rose Schiller, Virginia Blake Simonds, Mabel Grace Slocum, J. F. Stickney, Wallace Alexander Walter, Henry Weddle, and Lewis Edward Weston.

Diaries and Letters

Dysart Diaries, Rose Dysart, 1909–1918.

Seymour W. Tulloch, letter to daughter Marjorie, January 1916.

[Both held at the San Diego Historical Society.]

Other Accounts

Bellon, Walter. "The Inside Story of Hatfield's Flood," San Diego Historical Society.

Newspaper Interviews

Banks, Howard. *Star-News* (Chula Vista), January 1966.

Huston, Frank (water engineer). *San Diego Tribune*, December 1963.

Wolfe, Clara. *Star-News* (Chula Vista), January 1966.
Wueste, Rudolph. *San Diego Tribune,* December 1963.

Newspaper Archives
San Diego Union Tribune, December 1915–May 1916
San Diego Sun, December 1915–May 1916
Los Angeles Times, December 1915–May 1916

Books
Brocklesby, John. *Elements of Meteorology with Questions for Examination, Designed for Schools and Academies,* 1848.
Collinson, John. *Rainmaking and Sunshine,* Swan Sonnenschein, London, 1894.
Davis, William Morris. *Elementary Meteorology,* 1894.
Donaldson, Wayne. *Charles Hatfield: Pluviculturist Extraordinaire,* San Diego State University, 2000.
Fleming, James Rodger. *Meteorology in America 1800–1870,* Johns Hopkins University Press, 1990.
Halacy, D. S. *The Weather Changers,* New York, Harper & Row, 1968.
Higgins, Shelley J. *This Fantastic City of San Diego,* City of San Diego, 1956.
Hopkins, H. C. *History of San Diego: Its Pueblo Lands and Water,* San Diego, City Printing Company, 1929.
Humphreys, William J. *Rain-making and Other Weather Vagaries,* Baltimore, Williams & Wilkins Co., 1926.
Larson, Erik. *Isaac's Storm,* London, Fourth Estate, 1999.
Mason, B. J. *Clouds, Rain, and Rainmaking,* Cambridge, Cambridge University Press, 1962.
McGlashan, Henry Deyol and Ebert, F. C. *Southern California Floods of January, 1916,* U.S. Department of the Interior, U.S. Geological Survey, Washington, D.C., 1918.
Mills, James R. *San Diego: Where California Began,* San Diego Historical Society, 1985.
Pourade, Richard F. *The History of San Diego,* San Diego, Union-Tribune Publishing Company, 1960–65.
Schmid, Dorothy Clark. *Pioneering in Dulzura,* San Diego, Robert R. Knapp, 1963.
Smythe, William. *The History of San Diego,* San Diego, The History Co., 1908.
Spence, Clark C. *The Rainmakers: American "Pluviculture" to World War II,* University of Nebraska Press, 1980.
Stanford, Leland G. *Footprints of Justice in San Diego, and Profiles of Senior Members of the Bench and Bar,* San Diego County Law Library, 1960.

Journals
Patterson, Thomas W. "Hatfield the Rainmaker," *The Journal of San Diego History,* Winter 1970, Volume XVI, Number 1.
U.S. Department of Agriculture, Weather Bureau, *Monthly Weather Review,* 1905, 1906, 1933, Washington, D.C., 1905, 1906, 1933.